CLEOPATRA'S CONFESSIONS

A FELINE GUIDE TO COPING WITH DOGS, HUMANS, AND OTHER POINTLESS INTERRUPTIONS TO A GOOD NAP

By Cleopatra J. Cat

Skyhorse Publishing

Skyhorse Publishing books may be purchased in bulk at special discounts for sales promotion, corporate gifts, fund-raising, or educational purposes. Special editions can also be created to specifications. For details, contact the Special Sales Department, Skyhorse Publishing, 307 West 36th Street, 11th Floor, New York, NY 10018 or info@skyhorsepublishing.com.

Skyhorse® and Skyhorse Publishing® are registered trademarks of Skyhorse Publishing, Inc.®, a Delaware corporation.

Visit our website at www.skyhorsepublishing.com.

10 9 8 7 6 5 4 3 2 1

Library of Congress Cataloging-in-Publication Data is available on file.

Cover image by Thinkstock

Print ISBN: 978-1-62914-708-6
Ebook ISBN: 978-1-62914-905-9

Printed in China

AUTOBIOGRAPHICAL NOTE

I have occasionally been asked what the "J" stands for in Cleopatra J. Cat. It's a family name, from my mother's side, and it stands for Jarawandarla, which translated from the Siamese means: "none of your darn business."

CONTENTS

INTRODUCTION

Welcome kittens around the world! It is with great pleasure, and also a certain amount of sleepy indifference, that I begin the lofty endeavor of sharing my vast knowledge of cat life with you. In this book, it will be my mission to teach you all of the shortcuts, life lessons, and wisdom I have learned over the years, so that you can be better kittens, and one day, maybe even great cats. This will not be an easy task, especially since the mental effort involved will require me to take even more frequent and longer naps than usual. But, it is my mission all the same.

Despite being proudly antisocial creatures, we cats do end up sharing our space with other animals, frequently humans and dogs, so I think it's best to start with them. Humans have a purpose in this world: providing high quality cat food, both wet and dry; also the Minimum Daily Cat Requirement of petting, (no less than two hours); and most important, making available a good Sleep Environment for a cat. This must include comfortable chairs, couches, beds, countertops, and a variety of floor surfaces: bare wood, a cool cement area, linoleum, and carpeting. Carpeting is required not only as an Essential Sleep Option, but also for puking on. Never puke on anything not covered by carpeting.

Dogs, on the other hand, serve no useful purpose. All they do is disturb and disrupt, specifically disturb and disrupt cat sleeping activity. Fortunately, dogs can be trained. It's a nuisance, but it can be done.

Ideally, there would be no dogs, or they would be confined to an island somewhere in the South Pacific, where they could bark and run around to their hearts' content. But we don't live in an ideal world; we live in a world with dogs.

This book contains detailed tips on training your dog, but for starters, know that a couple of quick scratches to your dog's snout will have a very positive effect. Almost immediately, your dog will begin to approach you more calmly and cautiously.

I will leave details for upcoming chapters. For now, all you need to understand is that with proper training, both dogs and humans can rearrange their lives in ways which support you and your most important activity: sleeping.

Chapter 1
BASIC SLEEPING

In this introductory chapter we will only be discussing the most elementary techniques. You must walk, my kittens, before you can fly.

This cat is demonstrating a fundamental technique. Some might describe it as Heavy Napping, but I think it's simply Intense Regular Napping.

In your Intense Regular Nap you may opt for a Favorite Nap Location, but then you're limited by it. Suppose some careless human has put something down in your Favorite

Nap Location? Then what? My advice is: Be flexible. This cat has clearly flopped down on a Location of Opportunity, and is enjoying an Intense Regular.

Our next cat is demonstrating the Plain, or Uncomplicated Nap.

This is sometimes referred to as the No Frills Nap. Note the paw placement: high, chin level, near the whiskers.

Here is another Basic Napping Position:

We call this the Relaxed Afternoon. It appears that this cat is not alert, but she is quite capable of quickly and suddenly ripping her claw across the face of an intruder, any species at all. So be warned. Any cat should be able to throw a Relaxed Afternoon at any time of the day or night.

Hazards in the Way of Your Peaceful Naptime

A few unpleasant things to watch out for—not major threats, just nuisances to be aware of:

1. Vacuums – This horrible human invention does nothing special except make a lot of noise. Obsessive humans don't realize that any time you clean the floor, it just gets dirty again, so they spend a huge portion of their lives trying to present an ideal perfect floor with no natural elements. And because they are too lazy to clean anything themselves, they invent loud, obnoxious machines to do it for them. If you come across one of these beastly things (and you will), just try not to completely freak out. Get as far away from it as possible, but it won't do you any harm. Trust me, I have seen them all: the big bulky ones, the little dust busters, these new ones that drive themselves around the floor—I've been to battle with each and every one, and in the end, all that happens is I lose sleep. So, lose sleep you will, but that's about all.

2. Toddler humans – These are nasty creatures, apt to pull and yank at any part of your body they can get a hold of. The babies are alright—they can't do much

harm—but the toddlers are really sociopathic. They get pleasure in their size advantage and will make tormenting you as you nap one of their top priorities. The good thing is, they don't really know their own strength and are really just big scared oafs. Give 'em just a quick little warning bite, and they will go running to mommy. "OOOOOO, I'm so scared, the cat bit me!!! Mommy!!!" It's pathetic.

3. Slightly older children – The problem here is that they can and will pick you up. Observe:

This insolence will not be forgotten. You will pay for it someday, human, when you least expect it.

4. Lists – Lists are things that humans make, not cats, so in honor of this, I will not continue to work on this list anymore, and will instead take just a lil nap.

Okay, I'm back, did you miss me? That was refreshing—now, where were we? Right—nuisances. Let's talk about something related but slightly different—places we can get stuck! Yes, you will want to be very vigilant about climbing into, or attempting to nap in certain places in the house because, all of a sudden, these places can get closed off, and you can be there for a long time.

1. Closets – Yes, they are full of lots of strange things that are fun to explore. They are dark, mysterious, and downright irresistible. But, keep your ears alert, if a human comes near a closet and you are too deep in there to react, the door might get shut, and it can be a real waste of a day!

2. Garages – Again, full of fun things, maybe even mice and bugs to chase around, but if that garage door starts to close, you better be running because garages are not fun places to spend a week—trust me, I know.

3. Drawers – Great place to curl up for a nap. Oftentimes you can find a snuggly sweater or pajamas, which are great nap discoveries. But if you get yourself

too buried in there, and a careless human closes the drawer, it can be a real hassle. Once again, speaking as one who has been there and back.

4. Lists – Did I mention that we don't do lists? Right, so don't get stuck in one. As soon as you feel you are done with this list, go take a nap, as I will do myself at this time.

That was refreshing. Back to illustrative photos. This next picture illustrates a typical situation: a dog is sleeping where a cat needs to sleep.

This cat is thinking: *My best option is a four-point landing, claws extended, right onto this stupid dog's back. But I could set the stage by overturning the coffee cup in front of the couch, so that when I land on the dog and he jumps up howling, and runs away, he will be blamed for spilling coffee all over the floor. A more satisfying scenario, but requiring more work, and I don't feel much like working, so I think I'll just land on the dog with my claws now.*

Our next cat has taken charge of a human bed, and must not be disturbed. If humans want to sleep in the bed, they can do that only if they find a way to arrange themselves elsewhere in the bed so the cat doesn't have to move.

This cat is thinking: *I was here first. I have established position. If you want to be where I am, find another bed.*

And what do you think this cat is thinking?

This cat is thinking: *Yeah, go right ahead and pour some tea into that cup. Make my day.*

We will now take a short break for an impartial review of this book so far.

So far, this book is a big snooze! There's certainly nothing here that would interest a cat. A dog, maybe. A human? Who knows what interests a human? A telephone directory could interest a human.

Some Questions and Answers

Q: What's the best thing to sharpen claws on?

A: Furniture is the best. A case can also be made for curtains. A lace curtain, in particular. It's possible to jump fairly high up on a lace curtain, then ride it down with all four claws extended into the fabric. There isn't much actual sharpening going on here, but the overall experience is thrilling.

I found these curtains like this. Would I lie to you?

Q: Is there another photograph of a cat and some curtains?

A: Yes.

This cat is thinking: *I might miss the bird, but I won't miss the curtains.*

Q: What about those claw-sharpening posts they have at pet stores?

A: Those are no good. For one thing, half the fun of claw sharpening is that you're doing it on something you're not supposed to be doing it on. To sharpen on a post specifically designed for this purpose is undignified.

Q: Are there any cat toys available in pet stores that are fun to play with?

A: No.

Q: What about the cloth mice with the little bells on them?

A: No.

Q: Even the ones with catnip in them?

A: Those are better, but catnip shouldn't really be inside anything where you can't get to it. You should be able to roll around in it freely.

Q: How about the fishing-rod things with a feather suspended from it?

A: Better than the make-believe mice, but not as good as a string, and nowhere near as good as a ball of yarn that a human is trying to knit with. You can not only get the yarn, but also unravel the knitting. This is what play is all about. Play is spontaneous, it is not planned, and has nothing whatsoever to do with things humans buy in pet stores.

Eureka! The mother lode!

Oh, and by the way, human: thinking of buying me the $249 litter box shaped like a toilet? Don't do that. I won't use it. Instead, I

Final score: Cat 1, Couch 0

will piss and crap on your kitchen floor until you get rid of it.

Q: Specifically what kind of furniture is best for claw sharpening?

A: Anything that shreds is good. Sometimes a wood chair is acceptable, particularly if it's a very valuable antique because you can scratch right into the wood. But a rule-of-claw is that there should be some kind of upholstery going on so you can rip it up, which is satisfying all by itself, but also really helps with the sharpening.

Q: What about clothes?

A: Clothes can be satisfying as well, especially the more expensive kind. Dresses are among my favorites, also scarves. There's a gratifying ripping sound that the clothes make as you rip them.

Q: Won't the humans be angry?

A: Yes, and that's why it's a good idea to arrange to be someplace else when they discover the shredded clothes. If they can't find you, the anger dissipates, and there's time for them to adjust, and also wonder if maybe it was the dog that did it. Probably the dog *did* do it. Definitely.

Q: About the humans: sometimes there are humans who don't like cats. What can we do about them?

A: Many things. For example, if you have identified a human cat hater, find her bed, go there, and puke on her pillow.

Q: Is there anything else you can do?

A: Yes. Gradually work your way back into their good graces. Eventually, you will find your way into their lap. Crawl up into it, purr enchantingly, and when their defenses are down, pee. Maybe not quite as satisfying as puking on their pillow, but close. Very close.

Chapter 2
DOGS: WHY?

Bring it on, Fido.
Bring. It. On.

If it is your misfortune to have to share a home with a dog, there are a few consolations. The main one is that a dog does have a limited amount of entertainment value, but only if you can watch it from someplace a dog can't get to, like a shelf.

Photo of my friend Don Marritz with his dog, Greta, gazing up at him in a worshipful manner

v   Simply knock whatever's on the shelf off it to create the necessary space for you to position yourself there. The dog won't like the fact that you're up where he can't get to you, so he'll bark or whimper and jump around, which will make it easier for you to blame the dog for all the broken ceramics or whatever you had to sweep off the shelf to make the space available. A blank stare is all that's required while you watch the pathetic dog spectacle below. Maybe throw in a yawn and stretch. Drives them *crazy*.

Certainly life would be simpler and more peaceful if dogs did not exist. They serve no useful purpose. But humans want them around for unknown reasons. Maybe it's because dogs are so brilliant they worship humans. Seriously, they think their humans are gods.

Pathetic dog, in love with its human. Or just hoping that this look of love will lead to a hamburger.

It's too bad that we require humans to provide our food and Nap Locations. But you don't want to make an emotional connection with a human, or really any other animal, or even any other cat. A détente is possible, kind of like a treaty, but you can break it when you feel like breaking it.

It would be better if we got to select our humans rather than the other way around. But maybe "There aren't many differences between them." so really it makes little difference. The best you can hope for is a human who doesn't already have or will not ever get a dog. And a human who keeps your litter clean. If your litter is not kept clean, a little present left near but not inside the litter box will serve as a reminder.

A Review of The Dogma of Rufus

Speaking of dogs, a "colleague" of mine has written a guide to life for dogs. *The Dogma of Rufus*, by Rufus, an Old Dog. This book is almost unreadable and wrong in so many ways. Apart from the profoundly unsophisticated understanding of cats displayed in the book, the basic premise seems to be that that the central goal of life should be to obtain human food. As far as I can tell, this rambling, two-hundred-some page book is basically just a step-by-step guide to how to obtain their gastro-obsession.

I think where Rufus and I can agree is that the human food is interesting. At times, it can be different, tasty, and exciting. But it is hardly something to spend your life pursuing. I believe a far more meaningful life should be based around sleep. Rufus does touch on the subject of sleep, but his overwhelming distraction by human food makes it impossible for him to develop the theme completely.

In conclusion, this is a very terrible, not good at all book, which no species should read. But, what really could you expect from a dog?

More Thoughts about Dogs

It is quite likely that Rufus's misreading of a meaningful life goes beyond Rufus himself as a thinker, and extends to the entire dog population. I fear that a vast majority of dogs are under the veil of this very same human food mania, to the extent that they can barely see the good things life offers.

Dogs are very pathetic creatures. They have no pride or self-respect. Think about it—all the whimpering and begging that dogs do for human food, it's truly shameful. Cats do not beg. We are given food at the appropriate times, no questions asked. All the time dogs waste moaning and groaning, staring, and whimpering—if you have ever witnessed this display, it is really embarrassing. Of course while they waste away the afternoon obsessed with human food, we are enjoying a relaxing nap, or doing a little stretching, maybe mixing in a yawn or rolling and scratching our backs against a rough surface. By the end of the day, maybe the dog has achieved one or two brief moments of human food pleasure, but at what cost? We cats have spent an entire day living, being, enjoying.

Excuse me, but did you say, "We're getting a dog?"

The following cat is illustrating the concept of surprise mixed with disbelief:

Of all the stupid dogs on the planet, how did they find the stupidest dog in the universe? It is hard to fathom how this dog thinks I am going to allow it to put its ugly snout on my back and then go to sleep. I guarantee you that is not what is about to happen here.

Speaking of dogs, our next photograph illustrates "sleeping" and "cat," but it isn't the cat who is doing the sleeping. Once again, it is clearly an idiot dog who is sleeping and a cat who is looking extremely annoyed.

More Pathetic, Embarrassing Things About Dogs

You know what else is pathetic about dogs? How dependent they are on humans. Think of those dogs waiting sadly by the door when the humans leave to go out to dinner. Have you seen these dogs? Some of them just sit there for hours, waiting, praying that the door will open again and the humans will come back into the room. It is really painful to watch. Humans can be helpful at times sure, but to waste an entire evening, unable to exist without humans, is deplorable. And the way they totally freak out when humans walk into the room! Whimpering and running around in circles . . . it's just . . . I mean, I am running out of adjectives here.

What can you do to help the dogs with these problems? You guessed it! This is Not Our Concern (NOC). While it is embarrassing to witness, the fact that dogs are wasting their lives in this way is not something you should worry about. You need to focus on your own napping, stretching, and yawning. Do not get distracted!

Chapter 3
A PERSONAL CONFESSION

Okay. There was a certain period in my life when I was under a lot of stress. I'm not going to make excuses, but part of it involved a dog who was temporarily living in my house, doing what dogs do: disrupting, waking me from naps, eating my food, wanting to play. So, during this stressful period, I became addicted to catnip.

I'm not blaming anyone but myself, but I was hanging around with the wrong crowd of cats. Among them were strays, some ferals. I don't know where or how they got the stuff, but they just seemed to always have some around. I'd trade food for it. I'd trade anything for it. It made me forget, for a while, my own life. Catnip took me to a place that was always fun, always felt good.

Of course, when I'd used up what I had, I came crashing down. It was beginning to have bad consequences in my life. I stopped grooming myself, I wasn't getting in my sixteen hours of sleep. All I cared about was the next fix. Where, when, how?

If it weren't for the Intervention, I don't know what would have become of me. But there were cats I knew who cared deeply for me and saw what was happening. I was lured into a garage with the promise of catnip. Then the garage door closed, and I was surrounded by my friends, and they told me what was happening to me. At first, I tried to deny it, but they were relentless. I was overwhelmed.

I kicked the habit with their help, and the help of Catnippers Anonymous. They have a 12-Step Program, and it works. I'm just here to witness for you young kittens that while it's okay to indulge in a little social catnipping now and then, you have to do it responsibly. You must never let catnip become the focus of your life.

A Few Additional Questions

Q: Is a Siamese cat really a cat?

A: Yes. A cat with a lot of attitude. Not that there's anything wrong with attitude, it's what cats are about, but Siamese cats have even more attitude than regular cats.

Q: What is a Siamese cat thinking?

A: A Siamese is thinking: *I am descended from cats in Siam who were attended by human slaves. What the hell am I doing in Kansas? Where are my slaves? This is all a very big mistake. I want to speak with the manager. Hello? Where are my slaves?!*

Q: Are we really supposed to catch mice?

A: At one time we were, but not anymore. When humans got tired of hunting and gathering, they invented farming, leading to grain surpluses that had to be put in silos, which led to mice, and then *we* were hired to deal with the mice.

Q: Why don't we catch mice anymore?

A: We do still catch them occasionally, and it's very satisfying, but it requires a lot of stealth, quickness, and patience. You have to wait for them to come out, and they know you're waiting, so they won't come out. It's way too much work to do day in and day out, and depending on mice as your only food is simply unacceptable.

Q: How can we be sure our cat dish is full?

A: Make very unpleasant sounds until they put food in your dish. And it better be fresh!

Cat pointing out that her dish is empty.

Q: What is the best cat food?

A: The best cat food is the cat food you don't have. Humans are always trying to figure out which variety of cat food you like, so they can get it in large quantities and save money. Humans are extremely cheap that way. When they buy a lot of whatever you have previously selected, you change your mind. You now hate that food. They need to buy you something else. Keep 'em guessing.

Q: Is there also a large selection of different kinds of dog food?

A: No, because dogs are nitwits and will eat anything. There are a couple of different varieties, mainly to make the humans more comfortable. Dogs will even eat human leftovers, which is totally disgusting. But this book is not about dogs, and we shouldn't even be discussing them because it's such a distraction, like dogs themselves.

Q: Can't we also eat human leftovers?

A: It is undignified to eat human leftovers, but once in a while, if they're eating a particularly succulent variety of fish, not too highly spiced, we can make an exception.

Q: What is the best kind of kitty litter?

A: Once again: the kind you don't have. Just like with cat food, humans will try to figure out which brand is acceptable to you, then buy gigantic quantities of it so they can save a few bucks.

When you see a human staggering into the house carrying an enormous bag of kitty litter, that is the precise moment when you change your brand preference. Better to crap on the carpet than use that stuff.

That new kitty litter you just bought? I don't think so.

Chapter 4
INDOOR OR OUTDOOR CAT?
(HOW DARE YOU?)

The term "Outdoor Cat" is a misnomer. "Outdoor" merely refers to the fact that a cat can go or be either indoors or outdoors, when and if and how she chooses. A cat must have immediate access to both indoors and outdoors, and if this is not given immediately, you must insist on it relentlessly, if necessary. You know how to make horrible cat noises; you can make a mess. Do these things until you are given access to the outdoors.

Maybe you're thinking: this is not long enough for a whole chapter. It's long enough if I say it's long enough. If you'd rather read a book that has long, boring chapters, read another book. Probably the only reason you read is so you can fall asleep, since you don't have the ability we cats have to fall asleep anytime, anywhere.

Here is a human reading:

In any case, this chapter is now over, sorry if it's not long enough for you. Actually I'm not sorry. I don't care what you think.

Quick Facts about Us

Did you know that millions of cats are eaten every year in Asia? Of course, I find this disturbing, however, it would be hypocritical of me to be too outraged. Let's be honest, if we were five times as big as the humans, we would probably be eating them too. It's just the way the world works.

When cats chase their prey, their heads stay level, whereas dogs and many other animals bob their goofy heads up and down when they run. We are just so much freakin' better than dogs.

Cats make around one hundred sounds while dogs can make only around ten. Did I already mention how much more awesome we are than dogs?

The technical name for a hairball is a "bezoar" and the technical name for a group of cats is a "clowder." And, even more interesting, the technical name for the way humans waste all their time giving things names instead of living is "technical naming."

Cats were condemned as evil during the Spanish Inquisition (a period of time in human history in which humans did really stupid things for no good reason instead of just lying around and enjoying the afternoon—like most periods in human history). They were condemned as evil and killed, which lead to an increased rat population that helped spread the black plague. Mess with cats, and you will get yours.

Cats are North America's most popular pets. That means, more popular than dogs: seventy-three million cats, compared to sixty-three million dogs. Just to be clear, that is more cats, fewer dogs. Cats up, dogs down. Cats good, dogs bad. Just to reiterate, that's ten million more cats than dogs. That means that cats are approximately ten million times better than dogs.

Felicette "Astrocat" was the first cat sent into space. This happened because of the French. Just to be clear for any human readers out there—cats do not give a hoot about space. We aren't interested in even looking at outer space, let alone being shot into it. We are very happy, right here, on the rug, thanks very much.

About forty thousand humans are bitten by cats each year. I don't have any data on this, but, I am guessing about 99 percent of the time, the human deserved it.

According to the story of Noah's Ark, cats were created in response to Noah's prayer for the food he had stored on the Ark not to be eaten by rats. Thus, God made the lion "sneeze" out a cat. Now, I don't want to get personal here and offend anyone, but, humans are just so dopey. I mean . . . I just don't know where to start.

Cats' hearing is better than dogs'. Better than dogs, as in, superior. Like, more good.

Cats can run up to thirty-one miles per hour. I don't want to rub it in for you other animals out there, but, do you know how fun it is to run thirty-one miles per hour? Of course you don't.

Part of why cats rub up against people is to mark our territory with scent glands around our faces. Awww . . . And you thought we were being sweet.

When cats died in Ancient Europe, their owners held elaborate funerals, family members mourned by shaving off their eyebrows, and the cat was embalmed in a wooden mask and mummified. I personally think we should bring this one back. The least the humans could do is shave off an eyebrow or two. Is that too much to ask?

Cats have been known to give birth to up to nineteen kittens in one litter. Makes your octomom look pretty pathetic doesn't it, humans?

The first ancestors of the cats lived thirty million years ago and were known as "Proailurus," which is Greek for "first cat." Though it sounds vaguely familiar, this has nothing to do with *Prometheus*, which was just a really bad sci-fi movie. Okay, I just brought that up because I wanted to mention how much I disliked *Prometheus*. The characters were terrible!

Egyptians had a Goddess named Bastet, discussed at length elsewhere in this book, who had a woman's body and a cat's head. For my tastes, get rid of the woman's body, slap a cat body on there, and you've got yourself a pretty worshipable goddess.

Cats usually have about twelve whiskers on each side of their faces. Okay, I suppose only I would find that interesting, but, I just love us so much, I could talk about us all day long!

Cats are able to rotate their ears 180 degrees due to having thirty-two different muscles in our ears. This is something we willed into our evolution, basically so we could check out what was going on around the room without really having to wake up.

The Towser Tower was built in Scotland in honor of the cat Towser, who had caught over thirty thousand mice over a proud lifetime. Can I get a moment of silence please in honor of Towser? In fact, this calls for a moment of sleep. Let's all take a nap in reverence to Towser. Starting . . . now.

(These facts were gathered from www.randomhistory.com. Commentaries are exclusive property of Cleopatra.)

Chapter 5
SETTING MINIMUM ALLOWABLE PETTING TIME FOR YOUR HUMANS: ALWAYS ERR ON THE HIGH SIDE

Of course nobody can tell you what your Minimum Allowable Petting Time is. This depends on the cat. But I can offer some guidelines. For example: no less than two hours as a Rock Bottom Minimum. I'd say three, but I'm feeling unusually tolerant towards humans today, and it may be because they work most of the day and need to buy food for you, and possibly for themselves also, and do other things humans do, (who knows what?). So three hours might be a stretch for some of them.

Maybe you've just woken up from a satisfying three-hour Relaxed Afternoon Napper, and you're about to throw another one, maybe an Intense Regular, so you're feeling pretty good, str-e-e-tching out, and you feel yourself about to purr. Do NOT do this. At NO time can you allow the thought to creep into the human mind that you can purr without being petted. They like you to purr, it makes them feel relaxed—something they rarely feel themselves—so they must understand that the moment they stop petting you, you also stop purring.

Chapter 6
MAINTAINING MAXIMUM PAW SHARPNESS: SORRY ABOUT THE LACE CURTAINS, BUT THIS IS A SURVIVAL ISSUE

First, I want to reiterate the inappropriateness of scratching posts purchased by humans at pet stores. Why don't *you* scratch the scratching post, human?

You may want to give a scratching post a little exploratory rip or two when the humans aren't watching, but officially, you are not interested. They have just wasted more money on a useless cat toy. The ones with feathers attached to fishing rods do have a limited potential, and a ball with a bell inside: briefly amusing. But basically anything they get you at a pet store other than these items, and some really expensive cat food, which might be worth considering before rejecting: no.

Real play, as noted elsewhere, must be spontaneous, and should be initiated by you, not the humans.

Moving along: rugs are possible for claw sharpening, but they are difficult to damage, which is problematic. Gloves, especially fancy leather gloves, are excellent for claw activity, but if a careless human has left one lying around, you may have to compete with the dog for it. Get there first, before the dog finds out about it, then hide it. Only when the dog is at the park or asleep is it safe to take it from its hiding place and rip it apart.

Yes, it's tempting to pounce and rip, but much better to wait, to choose your time. The human pictured here thinks she is in control of the situation only because the cat is being so patient.

Another option is anything knit, like caps and sweaters. The previous cat is showing excellent patience. This moment is clearly way too early in the knitting process for unraveling to take place.

Also: scarves are good, but they shred too easily, so there's not much claw-sharpening going on there.

Paper: newspapers and magazines are good, but better are notes, phone messages, and recipes. Anything hand-written, in a collection called, "Grandma's Recipes" or "Family Favorites." Both provide excellent claw-sharpening material. And last but not least, let us not forget about those lace curtains, previously noted in an earlier Q&A, and included in this chapter's title. There may not be a lot of claw-sharpening here due to the minimal resistance of the lace curtains, but it is an undeniably thrilling experience to surf down the curtains, "Hanging 16," as the cat surfers say. After any satisfying claw-sharpening activity, you will want to take a nap.

Chapter 7
GIRL TALK: TEN TIPS TO TANTALIZE A TOMCAT

Okay, girls, I'm going to start right off with a confession: I don't actually have ten tips. But if you want to publish in *Feline Magazine*, you've got to say you have ten tips. It goes right on the cover, along with "Five P-u-u-rrrfect Ways to Prepare Catnip," and all those other teases. It's just the rules, I didn't make them up.

The main, basic way to attract a tomcat (and believe me, it ain't hard), is to advertise your readiness with a deep-throated, husky come-hither yowl. Then when he, or more likely they, arrive, wave your tail in the air fetchingly. That's all there is to it. Two tips. So much for the other eight tips. Forget about them, they won't be needed. Instead, we can move on to the next chapter. But first, an illustration:

Q: What happens after you have sex?

A: Kittens happen.

Q: How many kittens should a cat have?

A: Of course this depends on the cat and her circumstances. But as a rule of claw let's take a look at this cat:

Can't say for sure, but this gal looks like she's ready for some action.

This is too many kittens.

As I look at this cat with too many kittens, I'm thinking that the whole "Top Ten Tips to Tantalize a Tomcat" thing was maybe not such a good idea after all. Definitely time to move on to another subject.

Chapter 8
USEFUL LIES: YOU CAN'T TRAIN A CAT

*O*f *course* you can train a cat. But if you let your humans know this, they will immediately start training you to do things they want you to do that you don't want to do, and not to do things you want to do that they don't want you to do. Therefore, we all agree to perpetuate this nonsense that we can't be trained. For example, we use the cat litter instinctively. If we allowed them to think they were training us to

This is a female fitness trainer who is attempting to train an overweight cat, presumably to go on a diet or get more exercise or something. Take a look at the fitness trainer, then take a look at the cat, and *you* tell *me* who is going to win out in this confrontation.

do it, they'd start wanting to train us to come when they call, or chase Frisbees—God only knows where it would end. This next photograph, is, believe it or not, the only photo that is even remotely believable of a human trying to train a cat:

Dogs are so unbelievably brilliant that they actually *want* their humans to believe they can be trained. But of course they can't. About the extent of it is they will come if they're called, but in fact they will come if they're *not* called, so what's the point, exactly? Wait, I forgot: there's sit, lie down, roll over, and stay. That takes months and months of training, and really, when it's all done, the result is approximately the same as chance. There's also the humiliating, "beg." Some dogs will sit up on their hind legs if they think there's a scrap of food to get by doing it. These same dogs would kill their own grandmothers if they thought there was a scrap of food to be gained by it.

The following dog is trying to figure out what he's supposed to do to get the dog treat his trainer is offering. It is clear as day that this dog does not have a clue what he's supposed to do. Yes, he wants the treat, but what the heck do the humans want him to do? This dog illustrates the concept: lights on, nobody home.

Ohmigod, what do they want? Sit? Stay? Roll over? Lie down? What??!

So just remember: we cannot be trained. They must leave us alone so we can do more important cat things.

Chapter 9

OUR AFRICAN COUSINS: CHEETAHS, LEOPARDS, LIONS, TIGERS: WE ARE ALL CATS, WE HAVE THE SAME INSTINCTS, TURN YOUR BACK ON US AT YOUR OWN RISK, FRIEND

It is entirely appropriate that the collective noun for lions is a *pride* of lions. If you wanted to describe a cooperative group of cats, you would also use: a pride of cats. But we don't do cooperative groups. Or a committee of cats, which has more euphony, but we also don't do committees.

There are also schools of fish, we definitely do not do schools, and herds of sheep, and of course we don't do herds. It is called an exaltation of larks, but I guarantee there won't be that much exaltation if I get my paws on any of them. A sloth of bears is reasonably descriptive, a shrewdness of apes, on the other hand, is not. A charm of hummingbirds? Really? I am not charmed.

Additionally, a lounge of lizards (I swear I'm not making this stuff up), a mischief of mice (who will not be so mischievous if I get involved with them), and a nuisance of cats, which I find deeply offensive. But when we do further research, we find quite a few choices: a glaring of cats or a pounce of cats, which I find acceptable, and a destruction of cats which I like a lot.

Dogs, on the other hand, are described as a pack of dogs. Not that there are many dog packs running around most neighborhoods, but when they actually had to hunt for a living, they had packs, because they aren't smart enough to hunt on their own. More specifically, it's a cry of hounds. I would use, "an annoyance of hounds."

Aunt Emily. I just know if Aunt Emily lived close enough to me, she'd bring me delicious chunks of zebra and other delicacies.

I realize we've strayed a bit off topic here, but my point is that if you look at a few cats together as a pounce of cats or a destruction of cats, you understand why we are close cousins of lions, tigers, leopards, and panthers.

Here's a nice candid shot of cousin Ruth:

I feel a deep sense of kinship with cousin Ruth. Don't you?

According to Li Zhixing, a Chinese tiger expert, "There is a superstition here that a tiger will only attack you if you do something bad. Sometimes when people encounter a tiger, they don't run, they just pray."

I think it would be wise for any human encountering this particular tiger to pray, don't you? Li definitely has this thing figured out. No wonder the Chinese people are on schedule to take over the Earth.

And with all of them (the big cats), the females do the actual hunting, while the males lounge and sleep. This strikes me as wrong, but if you want something done right, you have to get a female to do it, never mind what species.

Chapter 10
GROOMING: NOT AS IMPORTANT AS SLEEPING, BUT THEN, NOTHING IS AS IMPORTANT AS SLEEPING

This seemed like a reasonable idea for a chapter way back when I wrote the Table of Contents, but it turns out that it was a lousy idea. There's really not a hell of a lot to say about grooming. So I'm not going to write this chapter. Instead, I think I'll take a nap.

If you're so interested in grooming, write your own chapter.

Chapter 11
HOLIDAYS

Christmas/Birthday Presents

It is important that you nip this concept of annual or biannual gift-giving in the bud—by means of complete rejection. Why is this? First, if your humans get in the habit of thinking that they can give you a gift just once a year, they will get the idea that they don't have to be 100 percent dedicated to your happiness the other 364 days of the year, which is totally unacceptable.

Second, with respect specifically to gift giving in celebration of human religious holidays, the idea that cats are going to get caught up in human mythologies and superstitions is laughable. This falls somewhere in line with the idea of wearing a witch's hat on Halloween—these are your holidays—we aren't into it, don't accept it. A cat is just not going to get all excited about the birth of some human two thousand years ago, or the rededication of some human temple by the Maccabees after its desecration by the Syrians (give me a break), or anything that involves fasting in some attempt to cleanse the soul and practice selflessness. Our souls are plenty clean—we lick them every day—and selflessness . . . just doesn't seem like something worth spending a lot of time cultivating.

Third, the gifts humans give us tend to be redundant. For example, a "cat bed." The humans think these snuggly little one-and-a-half foot ovals are going to be really exhilarating for us. First, thanks, but, I am fine with my human king size bed located in your bedroom. Second, we sleep wherever we feel like sleeping. It isn't something you can plan ahead for, pre-program, or assign to one space or another. Then you have your designated scratch-post type gifts. Once again, thoughtful, but completely redundant. As noted elsewhere, there is more than a sufficient amount of things already in the house that are fantastic for scratching—sofas, chairs, walls—we are fine with what we've got, so pass on the scratch post. Then, you have your high-technology, battery-powered mouse-type gift. This gives the humans the erroneous notion that they can just sit back with a glass of whiskey, feet up on the table, and watch their battery-powered mouse play with us all afternoon. This is not acceptable. Humans are required to put effort into playing with us, or it's just not worth our time.

Another problem with Christmas is illustrated by the following:

Yet another unanswerable question is: why do humans need to put ridiculous Christmas hats on us in celebration of what is supposed to be some kind of religious holiday? Does this cat look like a Jolly Little Santa Kitty now? I'm not seeing jolly anywhere.

So, how do we help the humans understand the futility of gift giving? Simply ignore any and all gifts presented to you. Okay, just so they don't think you are completely blind, you can whack at the electronic mouse once, but immediately after, turn away in complete indifference. You can give the scratch post a sniff or two, circle around it, and lean against it, but after that, you must never acknowledge its presence. Just sort of stare at the human who has given you the gift. It may take a few years, but sooner or later they will get the message.

Q: What if my human feels offended by my total and complete rejection of their gift?

A: You guessed it—that is Not Our Concern.

Q: Should I reciprocate this gift attempt by doing something nice for the human?

A: No.

Bringing Gifts for Your Humans

Okay, okay, instead of "no," I will go with "sort of." Because we don't waste our lives away chasing after unachievable, and ultimately, unsatisfying goals of wealth and achievement like the humans do, we don't have access to cash and credit cards. Therefore, we can't buy gifts. There is one gift that we can bring for our humans however, which requires no monetary investment. Why would we consider doing something for the humans, when it is clearly their responsibility to do things for us, for our pleasure and enjoyment exclusively? Because this one particular gift is as much fun for us as it is for them. I am of course talking about catching little mice and other critters to bring into the house as a show of appreciation. Why is it fun for us? Because we get to go out on the hunt! Explore the back yard for little rats, birds, and even freakishly oversized beetles, which are things the humans especially like to have brought into their homes. Why is it fun for them? As you will see, as soon as they see your gift, they too will engage in the fun process of chasing around this animal until they trap it. They will probably at that point take the critter back outside, which is basically them saying to you that it is your turn to go get it again and bring it back into the house.

But, that is it as far as us giving in to the humans, or showing affection for them. Don't get carried away and start thinking it's your responsibility to do nice things for your human—it is most certainly their responsibility to do things for you. So, one gift every once in a while and that's a wrap!

Cat Day

Look at all the pathetic human holidays they have, each one with its own parade. There's St. Patrick's Day, an excuse for the Irish to get drunk (as though the Irish ever needed an excuse), Columbus Day, commemorating the "discovery" of America by Christopher Columbus, who discovered that there were lots of native peoples who had already discovered America and were living there more or less in harmony with the environment, doing what humans do for recreation:

killing each other. Then there is Thanksgiving Day, where Americans celebrate the warm welcome they received from the Native Americans, who had the very poor judgment to welcome them with a feast, instead of killing them. Each of these holidays comes with a parade. There is even something called the Easter parade, which is only humans walking around in silly hats.

So instead of these unnecessary holidays, there needs to be Cat Day, and of course the Cat Day Parade. Various cat organizations would walk proudly down a big street, while everybody watches and waves, and there would be cat marching bands playing music.

Not really. Because, as noted elsewhere, cats don't do anything in groups, they certainly don't have marching bands, and would much rather be taking a long, afternoon nap. But that doesn't mean humans should not celebrate Cat Day with the Cat Day Parade. It would get them out of the house, while at the same time reminding them of how lucky they are to have cats. Maybe the cat food companies could sponsor floats, or maybe there would be huge, helium-filled balloons shaped in fanciful figures advertising one thing or another the way they have at Macy's Thanksgiving Day parade, a crushingly boring event which is only intermittently worth watching when one of the balloons is punctured and collapses on its holders and also a bunch of the spectators; or they lose control of it, and it floats up and away into the wild blue wonder.

These would be a few of the activities which would happen on Cat Day. It would be a lot better than Christmas, except even I will admit that I enjoy playing with the Christmas wrappings humans waste their time using to wrap up their dumb presents to each other. Once in a while they will get us a cat toy, and we can show our indifference to it by playing only with the wrapping. Also, I like the concept of an indoor tree, and ornaments I can knock off the tree and play with. So Christmas is a relatively good human holiday, but not as good as Cat Day would be.

Chapter 12
CAT MUMMIES OF ANCIENT EGYPT: IT WAS THE LEAST THEY COULD DO

It is well known that the ancient Egyptians honored their pharaohs by mummifying their remains and burying them beneath pyramids, so that humans could dig them up thousands of years later, unwrap them, and put them in glass cases in museums to frighten children.

What is less well-known is that they also honored their cats in this way. They held cats in such awesomely high esteem that they did to them what they did to their pharaohs.

In the spirit of full disclosure, I should also point out that they mummified their farm animals, too. Even their dogs. Why would anybody in their right mind mummify a dog? It can be argued that the ancient Egyptians were a few bricks shy of a pyramid.

Q: Are there photographs?

A: Yes!

Q: That's not a real mummy.

A: The real mummy is inside. This is a book for young kittens, I don't want to scare anybody. Anyway, you can clearly see how highly regarded the cat is who is inside this gold box with a statue on top!

Q: Are there other human people who had cat gods?

A: Scads of 'em. Really, there's hardly a human religion anywhere that didn't have cat gods. Here's one:

This is a pretty serious-looking cat god. If this one asks you to do something, do it.

Q: Are there others?

A: Get a load of this one:

I would approach this cat god very humbly and cautiously.

Q: Are there enough other cat god photos that you could write a whole other chapter called, "Cat Gods: Fabulous Feline Fotos You Can Worship Today!"?

A: That is an excellent question, and the answer to it is: Yes! Let's go immediately to that chapter right now!

Chapter 13
CAT GODS: FABULOUS FELINE FOTOS YOU CAN WORSHIP TODAY!

Q: Are you named after a cat god?

A: No, I am named after a fabulously rich and powerful queen of ancient Egypt who was the subject of not one, but two separate, famous plays by William Shakespeare.

Q: How did Shakespeare describe her?

A: "Age cannot wither her, nor custom stale her infinite variety."

Meet Bastet, Cat Goddess of Ancient Egypt. Bow down before her.

Q: Are we ready to move ahead with some more photos of cat gods?

A: Yes, we are.

Here's a nice one:

Not totally sure I get the hat, but it was a long time ago, and styles change.

Now, about this next one, I'm not necessarily saying I'd like to have to wear a gold necklace, but I'd appreciate the gesture:

Also, the earring is a nice touch.

Another appropriately worshipful statue of an Egyptian cat, with an appropriate amount of gold jewelry:

You might think this cat is too similar to the other one to add anything important to this book, but you would be wrong, as you always are. This cat is brown, the other was black. Also they are looking in slightly different directions. You can never have enough photos of cats wearing golden necklaces and earrings.

Here is a human child worshipping his cat, as he should:

Things would go much better for humans if they did a little less complaining and a little more cat worshipping.

Incredibly Pointless Dog Gods

I suppose to be fair, I should mention some dog gods as well, although there's no good reason to be fair. But just so you know: there were a few Incredibly Pointless Dog Gods as well as the Great Cat Gods You Should Be Worshipping Right Now. These were: Anubis, Bau (not kidding, this dog god's name was Bau), Fenrir, Kerberos (aka Cerebus), Kitsune, The Morrigan (probably a corruption of "The Moron"), Set (probably a corruption of "Sit! I said Sit, you dumb dog, not jump up and down!"), Wepwawet (winner: Most Pointless Dog God Name Award), and Xolotl.

Anubis, waiting to be fed.

Fenrir:

In this illustration, a Norse god is trying to chain Fenrir to a tree trunk. This is supposed to be a God, mind you, yet another god has to try to chain it, because otherwise Fenrir would eat all the other gods' food.

Okay, so Cerberus wins the Ugliest Dog God Award, which is really saying something. I think this dog god didn't really have three heads, he only seemed to have three because he was so annoying and he never shut up.

These are supposed to be dog gods, and yet they are abjectly cowering before some human. Can you imagine a cat god cowering in this way? Begging for food? Can you even imagine a *regular* cat doing this?

And now, mercifully, we come to the last of the dog gods, Xolotl, which sounds a lot like someone either hiccupping or puking.

This god was associated with lightning and death. How about: associated with barking, disturbing the peace, lightning, death, and smelling bad.

Okay. Well, that was a distraction. Back to more interesting stuff.

Chapter 14
HUMANS: SMARTER THAN BIRDS, NOT AS SMART AS DOLPHINS

Let's start off with birds. Birds do some things very well. For example, they can poop while flying, which is pretty amazing. Other than that, not too smart. For example, the canary. Humans keep canaries in cages, which isn't so great for the canaries, but I guess they don't mind it too much because they're always chirping. But even humans get sick of their chirping, so the humans put a small blanket over their canary's cage, and the canary stops. Suddenly, it's night! So the canary goes to sleep. Well, you know that's not how day turns into night. It doesn't happen that quickly, more of a gradual thing, where first, it gets darker. You'd think a canary might have noticed that, but no.

Not that I have anything against canaries. I like canaries, and would like to be friends. In fact, I always hope that the humans will leave the canary's cage door open while they go out for a few hours. The canary could fly out, and we could play together. Or if the canary is a bit shy, I could jump into its cage, and we could socialize right there! I think this would be fun for both of us. This next cat has clearly been socializing with a canary:

I think this cat and this canary had a really good time together. The cat probably opened the door to the canary's cage so the canary could fly around freely, maybe even out the window to join other wild birds in the, uh, trees. In the bushes and trees in the woods! It is now a feral canary.

I realize this is a bit of a digression, but the whole cat/canary thing brings to mind the expression "the cat that swallowed the canary." This is what humans use to describe a feeling of complete satisfaction, a feeling they rarely, if ever, achieve. In fact, they are so fascinated by the cat/canary dynamic that they invented a whole cartoon, *Tweety and Sylvester*, about a cat and a canary. I've never understood why Sylvester never ate Tweety. Some cats who discussed this with me have suggested that it was probably something in the contract Sylvester had to sign. Really? In the contract? Screw that. I just ate Tweety. Sue me.

But this chapter is supposed to be about humans, really the canaries were only an example of something that humans are smarter than. On the other hand, there isn't much evidence that humans are smarter than dolphins, and in fact quite a lot of evidence suggests they are not. Also whales. Humans may be smarter than sharks, but you have to admire sharks because they are extremely focused, which humans aren't. A shark is not easily distracted, especially if there happens to be blood in the water, caused by probably, a shark bite.

But again, we're getting distracted. Actually, I like humans. If I were ten times bigger than them, I wouldn't necessarily kill and eat them. However, that *is* a pleasant subject for a daydream in my mid-afternoon nap. If you've ever watched the Discovery Channel (and who hasn't?), you have admired the speed and grace with which a cheetah catches up with and kills her prey.

Here's a shot of my cousin, the cheetah, in action:

Those gazelles are pretty fast, but my money is on the cheetah.

But a human would not pose enough of a challenge, really. Where's the sport?

So we're not going to imagine chasing and bringing down a human, and eating one, although if I were big enough to do that, I would make sure I left enough for the hyenas and the other animals who do clean-up. Also the vultures. Because cats are considerate. After we've had our share, all are welcome to the human carrion.

But we were talking about humans who are alive, not human carcasses we might have killed. Unlike canaries, live humans have big brains, with which they solve problems. Unfortunately, most of the problems they solve are problems they themselves have created, so that's kind of a wash. Here's a famous human problem solver:

You may wonder why we have to settle for a not-good stamp from Malawi instead of any of the recognizable photographs of Einstein, but his family probably has the rights to all of them and they're selfishly charging a lot of money for them. Anyway, what Einstein solved was the problem of the relationship between matter and energy, and guess what? Solving that problem only led humans to a lot bigger, worse problems with nuclear weapons, with which they will probably kill themselves, and us, and dogs, and horses also. I'd be fine with a nuclear weapon that only killed all the dogs, but we don't have one of those yet.

At this point, you may be wondering: what purpose do humans serve? They do, actually have a purpose: to provide food and a variety of excellent sleep location options for a cat. Another important function is to pet a cat. While humans are petting you, purring is permitted. The moment the petting stops, you stop purring. It's not a free service, it's something humans enjoy, which you trade for the petting. If you give it away, you won't get your Minimum Basic Allowance of Petting (MBAP). The following cat is getting proper attention from her human:

Here's the deal, human: you keep scratching my head, I keep my claws retracted. Don't make me dig them into your knee, which I could totally do if you stop, or if there's anything lacking in your technique.

Other than feeding and petting cats, humans have no purpose. It is a mystery why they are always running around, very upset about some petty human issue, typically a waste of time. There are, for example, an almost infinite variety of Family Issues. Disputes between husbands and wives, between parents and their children, between the children, between the parents and *their* parents, on and on it goes. The following is a typical human family interaction:

Instead of fighting over potato chips, they should be trying to select a particularly delicious brand of cat food for me. I recommend the most expensive brand, I'll decide later if I'll eat it. Probably not.

Brothers and sisters are still quarrelling with each other when they are adults! All of this disturbs cat sleeping activity, and can be almost as annoying as dogs running around, barking and disrupting your nap.

Here's another typical human family interaction:

While brother and sister fight, Mom is considering Valium, and also wondering where Dad is. You can bet when Dad reappears, she's going to let him have a piece of her mind. If it's soon, everyone will be fighting at the same time, which at least has some comedic value for a cat, situated in a good Sleeping Location above the humans.

Kittens play with each other briefly when they're very small, but after that it's every cat for herself. Other cats are only competition for a limited amount of food, sleep locations, and petting. Humans have only a pitifully small amount of time to devote to petting a cat, and if there's another cat around, that time can be cut in half!

However, humans also have made tremendous contributions to the well-being of all life on Earth. It's just that right now, under pressure as I am, I can't think of any. I'm quite sure they will come to me, but just to change things up here, let's go on to a new subject, and we'll come back to the outstanding human contributions to life on Earth in a later chapter.

Chapter 14A
MORE THOUGHTS ON HOW GRACEFUL WE ARE AND HOW BUNGLING THE HUMANS ARE

It seems worth elaborating on this topic. You may have noticed that the bungling, floundering, graceless nature of the humans can be disturbing to say the least to our sleep. Say for example, you are sleeping on the floor, and one of your humans comes stumbling into the room; unfortunately for you, you have to be alert to where they step. They do not have the sophisticated, evolved sense of space that we have, and may even step on you with their bulky, weighty, unnecessarily large and awkward bodies. Of course, we cats know at all times where we are, where we are gently stepping, and definitely who may be sleeping in the general area, so we do not have this problem. But the humans do. So don't get too comfortable in any one space. If at any time you hear a human oafishly wobbling around in your direction, you must be on alert! Okay, you don't have to be on high alert, you can just sort of lift an ear, as the bumbling humans are far too slow to actually pose much danger. As long as your ear is pointed in the direction of the humans, you will have little problem gracefully avoiding their artless, flopping legs and feet.

Even More Thoughts on Our Total and Complete Gracefulness

We also do not fall from things. We may be bumped off, say for example, a living room mantel or a bookshelf by a stumbling, awkward human, but we would not fall off by our own doing. And even if we were to be bumped off of such a location, we would manage to recover our balance mid-air and land smoothly on our paws. The humans, however, cannot sleep on bookshelves or other high places because of their aforementioned oafishness. They would likely roll over in the middle of a dream for example and go crashing to the floor. Furthermore, they would not realize that they were falling until they landed on their heads, and certainly would not land gracefully on their feet. This is why humans do not sleep on high places like mantels and bookshelves. This pleasure is exclusively ours.

Sleep Deprivation and the Human Condition

Why are humans the way they are? There are many words that we may think of when we describe humans, among them—oafish, slow, not much to look at, and rather stupid. But why are they so? As frustrating as some of their characteristics may be for us at times, we must have some sympathy (some), considering the haze of sleep deprivation in which they live their lives. Imagine how you would feel if you were limited to seven hours of sleep per day! How would you look if you only took somewhere between zero and one nap per day? Probably not so great. Considering how little the humans sleep, it is amazing they are able to function at all. One of the many things the humans are wrong about is their understanding of sleep. To break down the logic for you, humans believe that the waking state is more productive than the sleeping state, and so they actively and intentionally limit the amount of sleep they engage in. This is of course insane, but that is what they believe.

You tell me: Does this look like a good night's sleep?

They think that if they work all the time, constantly engaging in activities during the wakeful state, maybe one day there will be some reward for this. Who knows what they think this amazing reward that validates living a miserable, sleepless life is going to be, but whatever it is, they never get the reward. Furthermore, they try to structure their sleeping and waking states to fit in with some ideal human sleeping and waking schedule. This means that when they feel tired, they don't necessarily go to sleep, and they wake up when they don't actually feel like waking up.

The word "dumb" doesn't quite capture it, but, it will have to do for now.

When we cats feel tired, we sleep. It really isn't that complicated. When we feel like waking up, we wake up. We lead a purpose driven life, and when we decide to stop sleeping, it is because we have something very specific we want to do. The humans wake up, force themselves out of the sleep state preemptively, and then sometimes ask themselves: what should I do now? Or they consult their agendas for ideas of things to do. It seems to me that if you have to consult an agenda about what it is you should be doing, it probably isn't something very urgent, and could certainly wait until the sleep state has come to a natural end.

In any case, this is part of the reason why humans are so slow, graceless, and physically unattractive. What can you do to help?

Are you thinking about ways that we cats can help the humans sleep better? If so, you have answered the question incorrectly. Why? Because that was a trick question. The humans and their problems are Not Our Concern (NOC). Maybe if you were a dog, you would think briefly about how you could help your human sleep better, or maybe relax more, appreciate life or whatever, but that is not what cats do. We must at all times be concerned with our own situation.

Do not waste time worrying about the humans. You must always be vigilant about your own sleep, your own waking states, and your own general happiness. There will be other moments throughout this book in which you will be tested on this subject, so be attentive!

Chapter 14B
COMMUNICATING WITH HUMANS

Communicating with humans is enormously difficult, because they are incapable of understanding the most obvious messages we send them. We send these messages with our changing facial expressions, which they are unable to read, also with the infinite variety of sounds we make to express our feelings and communicate our wants and needs.

Why can't they understand us? Who knows. They profess to be interested in us, and are constantly speculating about what we want. What we want is plain as the noses on their faces. We demonstrate it with our body language as well as with our voices. But they are incapable of understanding the simplest things we say. Even dogs get the basics. Can you imagine any sentient being more obtuse than a dog?

The following image illustrates the animal that a human is stupider than:

I'll be the first one to admit that the first word which springs to mind when you look at this photo is "ugly," not "stupid." This dog makes Winston Churchill look like Brad Pitt. This is a profoundly ugly dog, but that doesn't mean he is also not stupid. He looks pretty stupid to me.

It's tempting to make the effort to comprehend why humans are so deficient in the basic skill of understanding cat communications that we have to compare them unfavorably to dogs. But to comprehend it would require a lot of thought about humans, and they really aren't worth the trouble. They have their purpose, as explained elsewhere in this book. It is to provide us with food, shelter, our Minimum Basic Daily Requirement of Petting, a variety of beds and carpets to puke on, and many different but excellent Sleeping Locations. Beyond that, they are quite useless. We ourselves have to do the work of sweeping away their expensive trinkets from bookshelves, mantels, and other perching areas from which we can gaze down on them and their dogs. We also have to knock over their glasses of ice water and sometimes their vases full of cut flowers to get any decent drinking water. If humans have any purpose on Earth besides what I have just mentioned, I can't think what it is right now, and more important, I feel a nap coming on.

So this will be another short chapter, the best kind.

Chapter 15
INTERMEDIATE SLEEPING

Now that you've mastered Basic Sleeping, you're ready for Intermediate Sleeping, and the very first skill to develop is identifying an Intermediate Sleep Location. Basic Sleep Locations are just wherever you are at a given time. Flop over, close your eyes, that's all there is to it. But an Intermediate Sleep Location (ISL) is usually on top of something: a piano, a TV, a wardrobe closet, a high shelf inside a closet, which has maybe shoes or hats you need to clear off so you can seize the location, or in military terms: the objective. An even better ISL is on a high shelf of a bookcase, normally occupied with books, sometimes carved book stops, and even expensive vases. These must be swept off the shelf to prepare the ISL for you. It's best if you can arrange to blame the smashed vase on the dog, which is the only useful function a dog has, providing a blaming opportunity for whatever you have to break.

This cat has found a nice ISL in a bookshelf. She is looking down, with satisfaction, on the broken remains of vase or statue she had to clear away in order to secure the space.

Here is another cat after securing a good ISL:

Yeah, about those figurines that were on the shelf I'm on? You'll find them in pieces on the floor. You can glue them back together if you want, but find someplace else to put them. This shelf is mine.

One of the best things about an elevated ISL is that you can observe humans and dogs undisturbed from on high, and also avoid that great insult to peace and quiet, the vacuum cleaner—arguably the worst human invention ever. Most human inventions, and especially those they are most proud of, make a lot of noise, and some of them, like the vacuum cleaner, also move dangerously. Other human inventions that make noise include airplane engines, motorcycles, which are intentionally noisy, and jackhammers. Humans make a lot of noise with big cement-making trucks, which make cement they pour someplace. Then when it's dried, they suddenly decide they don't want it where they put it, but it's too late now, so they have to use jackhammers to bust it up and cart if off to the dump. Another stupid, noisy invention is the amp, used to amplify the mildly unpleasant sound of a guitar into a humongous wall of sound that is so loud that the teenagers who are making it have to protect themselves from the noise they're making with noise-blocking earphones. It never occurs to them that instead of cranking the amp up to fifteen and then putting noise-blocking earphones on to protect themselves, they could turn their amps down to maybe six or seven.

At least an amp is not also moving while it is making noise. Cars do move. Nothing good has ever happened to a cat who is forced to ride in a car, usually in a cage. Only two places you end up: one of them is the veterinarian's office, a torture chamber where you are manhandled and abused. Take a good look at the cat on the vet's table. Does this look like a happy cat, or a cat who is being abused? And while you're looking at the cat, look at the vet. That is an evil smile if I've ever seen one. He's thinking, *How much more pain can I inflict on this cat, and how much money can I charge this stupid woman for it?*

The other car trip is one out into the country where you're abandoned and left to survive on your own as a feral cat, something for which you have not been trained.

If your car trip is so you can be abandoned in the country, and you manage to survive, you have to hunt your own food. The whole hunting-killing thing is fine in theory, but when it's necessary for survival, it's way too much trouble. Better to let the humans feed you and watch the Discovery Channel for vicarious hunting-killing experiences.

Chapter 16
PUKING: WHERE, WHY, WHEN, AND HOW

So you're going to puke. The first question is: where? The very best place to puke is on a white shag rug; the deeper the shag and the whiter the white, the better. But you may not be fortunate enough to have that opportunity. The next best thing is a deep shag rug of any color, and then any rug. But if it's just a puny little rag of a carpet, you must consider chairs, couches, and beds, for these can also be excellent puke locations.

We're actually not going to have a lot to say about the next question: why puke? Why is because you're a cat, and because you can.

As for when, the best time is at night. For one thing, you are at your best, since you're a nocturnal animal, and humans are at their worst, because they are not. They are not alert, and don't see well, so you can lay a nice, big puke down on the way to the bathroom. They won't see it, but they *will* feel it. It's just one of those unforgettable feelings, stepping in fresh cat puke. Hopefully it will be on some carpeted area. Usually, it will startle them and cause them to cry out, waking others. There isn't a lot that compares with this in terms of sheer entertainment value. Sometimes, if it's a male human who has stepped in your puke, the male will try to get away with merely wiping the puke off his foot and sneaking back to bed, so you may have to yowl a little to make sure the female is alerted, so she will make the male actually clean up the puke from the carpet.

You can use puking to send a number of different messages to the humans. For example, the most popular message is:

1) That cat food you just bought? I don't like it.
   Another frequently-used message is:

2) The baby you brought back from the hospital? I don't like it, take it back.
   And one of my personal favorites:

3) I have not been getting my Minimum Daily Allotment of attention.

4) But puking can be message-free. Puke for the simple joy of it. I am a cat, therefore I puke.

Some More Questions & Answers

Q: I read in *Harper's Index* that 58 percent of American cats are overweight. Is that true?

A: That is nonsense. You can't believe everything you read in *Harper's,* and most likely, you can't believe *anything* you read there.

Q: But maybe if we got more exercise . . .

A: Exercise is not a cat concept. It's a human concept, a dog concept. Cats are way too busy sleeping. An occasional sudden move to pounce upon and kill a careless mouse or bird is all the exercise we require.

Q: Are all kittens adorable?

A: "Adorable" is not a word I use. It is the function of all baby animals to be adorable, so the adults will want to have more. But for example, I do not find puppies adorable. They are merely learning how to be dogs, which takes forever because they're dogs, and really stupid.

Q: But about kittens . . .

A: Okay. Kittens *are* adorable. So adorable that I'm writing this book entirely for kittens. But they have no dignity until they become cats. They need to be adorable as kittens so humans will adopt them, but after that's done, there's no reason for further adorableness, so they can let that go, and the sooner the better.

A: Can we see some photographs of adorable kittens?

Q: There are millions of photos of kittens on the Internet. If you think I'm going through more than a couple of pages of them, you're a few yards short of a ball of yarn.

A: Please, just a couple?

Q: Okay, if you'll stop your mewling, I'll find a couple. Really they're all the same.

I'm telling you, if you've seen one adorable kitten, you've seen them all.

Q: Just one more adorable kitty photograph, *please?*

At least there might be something interesting going on with this one other than adorable, but what, I don't know. Maybe this kitty is seeing a helpless bird caught in a bush? Could be something like that. And now we're going to move on.

Q: What noises should I be able to make as an adult cat?

A: Your Basic Communications Arsenal must include the yowl and the hiss. The yowl can be an invitation of sorts, or a complaint, directed at humans, dogs, or other cats. The "meow" is an invention solely for humans, as a greeting or a demand for attention.

Q: Can these be illustrated?

A: They can be. Observe:

To be honest, it's not that easy to illustrate a yowl. You kind of have to be there. But hissing is easier:

This cat is clearly making a statement. She does not like something that has happened. Whoever has offended her had better fix this situation ASAP.

Pop Quiz

Here are two animals. Which one do you think knows what she's doing and which one doesn't have a clue?

I'm not giving any hints. If you can't figure this out on your own, you have flunked this quiz.

Here are two more animals. Which one is happy, and which one is not?

If you don't get this one right, you fail the entire book.

Here's another shot of two animals, one of whom is clearly furious at the loss of dignity she is suffering because she's been forced to wear human clothes. The other animal hasn't the wit to be furious or the dignity to lose.

Animal on the right: If I could, I would go for your jugular right now. Animal on the left: Duh?

And now, back to: What is this cat thinking?

You want to use this sink? Sorry, it's occupied. Find another sink.

This sofa? Also mine. But I'm sure you can find another one. Humans are so resourceful.

Who is this?

This is a famous Italian relative of mine. Looks a little bored, like she's tired of posing for the sculptor and is not too sure what the shield is all about. If I were the human sculptor, I'd hurry up. It's not a long way from bored to annoyed, and you don't want this cat to be annoyed with you.

Essay question: Why is this cat angry?

Use your imagination, but support your theory with whatever evidence you can manufacture.

Chapter 17
NAP TIME

You might suppose from the title of this chapter that it will be about the right time to take a nap, or how long a nap should last. But that's not what this chapter is about. This chapter is about how it's time to take a nap right now. So we will be doing that starting immediately.

Chapter 9

Chapter 18
EXPOSING THE INTERNATIONAL DOG CONSPIRACY

There could hardly be a more urgent subject than Exposing the International Dog Conspiracy. However, this chapter came right after Nap Time, an even more urgent chapter, so we slept through this one also. In fact, we're probably going to nap right on through the next chapter. Because, number one on the list is: Get More Sleep. So we'll be taking our own advice, and you won't be hearing anything more about the other nine things on the list.

Test: What *Is* This Cat Thinking?

This is a fun, easy quiz. First look at the photograph, then see what the cat is thinking underneath.

The cat is thinking: *If this big, dumb dog doesn't get his paw off of my back in the next five seconds, he is going to regret it big time.*

What is this next cat thinking?

This cat is thinking: *I will wait until the human has knitted more of that sweater, possibly until it's almost finished, before I attack and destroy it. There's no hurry.*

How about this one?

This cat is thinking: *Yes? And you woke me up because . . . ?*
This better be good, human.

And this next cat? What is she thinking?

This cat is thinking: *Well, I know these fish are not for me.*
I'm just watching over them, guarding them from a potential
thief. Maybe, as a preventive measure, I'll eat them proac-
tively. Get ahead of the curve.

About those curtains: It was a survival
issue. Sorry (not really).

Yeah, so this photograph is officially the Cute Cat Photo of 2014. Guess what? It's not at all cute. In fact, it's not even a little bit cute. It's a photograph of a cat prisoner of war. I'm thinking it's Exhibit A in our War Crimes trial. You want to own up to that? I'll see you in prison with Milosevic in the Hague.

Our next cat illustrates the point that there is, contrary to popular belief, Cat TV. It's not like the hugely uninteresting human TV. It's completely interactive:

This cat is thinking: *I love this program! This is my favorite program. I love it so very much that I think I'm going to eat it.*

Speaking of eating:

Could it be that the cute little sparrow on the next branch is totally unaware of my presence? That would be very unlucky for the sparrow, but very lucky for me. Must stay perfectly still, perfectly still . . .

This next cat has probably seen too many movies.

You talkin' to me? Are you talkin' to me?

The next photo illustrates the fallacy of "the fat cat."

The "fat cat" is an invention of veterinarians. This cat is merely well-fed.

Also this cat:

You got something to say to me? Maybe some smart comment on my weight? Go ahead. But after you've said it, don't go to sleep again, ever.

Our next cat is engaging in the constitutionally protected act of claw-sharpening.

Step 1: Settle into comfortable position on couch. Step 2: Extend claws. Step 3: R-r-r-r-i-i-i-i-i-ppp!!

Here is a cat thinking quietly about a dilemma.

I totally need to knock this street lamp into the street, but I can't get to it. Maybe if I lean way over I can reach it. If I can do that, it will smash into a thousand pieces, maybe even start a fire. That would be fun!

Unlike humans and dogs, cats are not concerned with gathering possessions. Dogs of course, are mainly concerned with bones, which they bury, then forget where, so they have to dig up everything everywhere. Humans devote their entire lives to gathering possessions of all kinds, whether they have any use for them or not. However, occasionally, possession can become a cat issue:

These cat treats? They are *my* cat treats, not yours. Do not even *think* about trying to take them away from me or you will be very, very sorry.

Chapter 19
CATS IN THE MEDIA

There are other myths that aren't so much part of common culture, but rather are cynically perpetuated in the media. Stereotypes and cheap, punch line humor in print and visual media offer vastly misleading ideas about cats. For example, we may lick at a piece of lasagna, but, we would never eat a whole plate of this or any other vile human food. There are some basic elements of human food, which are okay—turkey, butter, some other meats—but the way they pile all of these elements up together and smother it up in spicy or sweet sauces is not something we approve of. Also, the idea that we would ever be outsmarted by a mouse, as frequently portrayed in a particularly tasteless "comedy" duo TV series, is ridiculous. We don't slobber and spit when we speak, nor do we use catch phrases like "sufferin'" whatever!

Then you have your catwoman kind of situation. The reason I say "situation" is because unbeknownst to most humans, there are whole series of cat/human blended super-heroes. The idea itself is ridiculous. This fictional, preposterous amalgamation is a total one-way trade—the human gets to integrate all of our excellent cat abilities, and what do we get in exchange? Just a great big pile of human problems: having to save the world, deal with plotting, bizarre, also freakish enemies, unrealistic love/hate romantic misadventures, and poorly written box office flops.[1] Catwoman isn't alone—there was also *Miss Fury, Princess Pantha, The Black Lion,* and even, *The Adventures of CatMan,* (it was from Australia, but still). All of these are the production of human fantasies that somehow, by some not very logical series of events, a human will become part cat. But, can you really blame the humans? What sentient being wouldn't want to be more catlike, even if it is the result of inconsistent, implausible, and often not even really explained circumstances?

The humans tend to spend a lot of time longing to be something better than humans. They have their Centaurs, which are half human, half horse; their Satyrs, which are half human, half goat; and even Onocentaurs which are half human, half donkey. Cats, don't worry about these kinds of things. We have better things to do. There isn't a lot of crime in the cat community (we don't steal anything that isn't edible),

---

[1] *Catwoman*, a 2004 superhero movie staring Halle Berry, was the masterpiece final production of a medly of rewrites involving twenty-eight different screenwriters and was declared "arguably the worst superhero film ever made" by the *Orlando Sentinel*.

and what little there is, we deal with it internally, without the need of a masked, flying super-mutt.

Cats in the News

It's not every day you open the newspaper and learn something new about cats. Recently, however, fossils were discovered in China that prove cats were present 5,300 years ago, doing our thing alongside ancient humans. The find, according to Fiona Marshall, a zooarcheologist at Washington University in St. Louis, was "very unexpected." It wasn't that unexpected among the cat community, but humans are constantly surprised by cats. Another zooarcheologist, Melinda Zeder, an expert on animal domestication at The Smithsonian Institution's National Museum of Natural History in Washington, DC, had this to say: "The impact of domestication is difficult to tell from archeological remains. Actually, it's hard to tell when you have the living damn cat, because they retain so much of their native behaviors." You got that right, Melinda. It's hard to tell when you have the living damn cat. We retain all our native behaviors, and give nothing up whatsoever. Why would we give anything up?

I think there ought to be a statue of Professor Zeder outside The Smithsonian in Washington. Or maybe when she passes away, she should be stuffed and put inside one of those dioramas that they have in museums, where she could be posed looking at some cat bones. Not sure what else would be in the diorama, maybe a few other stuffed scientists. Normally, you don't expect human scholars to be quoted swearing in the newspapers, but most human scholars don't study cats. Those who do, I imagine, swear like sailors and drink like Irish poets on a book tour.

The following photo may or may not be a wax statue, but I think it's probably what Professor Zeder looks like, more or less, so it would be a good model for a statue, which could be outside The Smithsonian. I know they would attract a lot more visitors if this was outside.

Professor Zeder, captured in a candid moment at the 2014 International Conference of Zooarcheologists in Zurich, Switzerland.

Well, finding a model for the statue of Professor Zeder to be erected outside The Smithsonian in Washington has taken us on of a bit of a digression from the basic subject here, which is cats in ancient China. Naturally we were in ancient China, since we were in ancient Everywhere. There were no dogs in ancient Everywhere, they came later, I think humans raised them to slaughter and eat, not a bad idea, really. But we were helping the ancient Chinese with their mice problem, so they became attached to us, and we've been there ever since. So that concludes Cats in the News for today. Go, and sleep.

Chapter 20
MORE CATS IN THE NEWS

According to an article that appeared in the March 12, 2014 issue of the *Los Angeles Times,* and probably in quite a few other newspapers in the US, Canada, the UK, and Europe, a man in Portland, Oregon was forced to call 911 because the family cat, Lux, a twenty-two-pound Himalayan, had the man trapped in his own bedroom. The cat, who apparently was moody to begin with, scratched the human's seven-month-old child. The man kicked the cat, who then turned on him, chasing him into the bedroom, and remained outside the locked door, yowling with rage. The man was terrified and called 911. He described the cat to the emergency dispatcher as "very, very, very hostile." He told the dispatcher that Lux "had a history of violence," according to audio obtained by the *Oregonian,* a local newspaper. After discussing the situation with a supervisor, the 911 operator called the police, who arrived with a dog snare, with which they captured the cat, freeing the man.

I certainly don't advocate attacking your human, but in this case it was clearly a case of self-defense. The human admitted that he kicked the cat. A human will sometimes kick a dog, but most dogs will not defend themselves or retaliate. But a cat has more sense. You have to establish boundaries. A human may not be permitted to kick a cat. So Lux did the right thing. The human is very lucky he managed to escape and lock himself in the bedroom. It could have been a lot worse for him.

Humans erect statues for their heroes. I think Lux should have a bronze statue made in his honor, and placed in a prominent location in Portland, Oregon. Maybe at the entrance of their famous Rose Gardens. An inscription in Latin would be appropriate, something that translates to, "Enough Is Enough." Maybe the date, March 11, 2014 carved into bronze below.

Even More Cats in the News

Another great story, and you can see this for yourself if you go to YouTube and search for "Hero cat saves young boy from dog attack in Bakersfield, California." It's pretty dramatic, and I can't describe it adequately, but we're talking about a little four-year-old boy (Kevin) on a tricycle, a vicious dog, and a heroic cat (Tara) who attacks and chases the dog away in a matter of seconds! This is a MUST SEE!!

Chapter 20A
THE ILLUSTRATIVE CASES OF BLACKIE AND TINKER

Blackie is the richest cat in history. He was left $25 million dollars in inheritance when his owner, Ben Rea, died. Tinker was a simple cat who wandered into an old woman's home, made friends, and was left $160,000 in inheritance.

If you think about these cases enough, some of the problems with the human condition become very clear. Humans go through life dreaming and yearning for one thing or another. If they get one of the things they want, they quickly move onto another. Nothing is ever enough for them. The way they simplify their unquenchable yearning is to put it all into monetary form. I want to make more and more money so that one day I can be happy. If I make this great fortune, then all of my dreams will be satisfied, and I can live in peace.

Now, let's look back at Blackie and Tinker. What would a cat do with all the purchasing power and financial stability a cat could ever dream of? Here are a few things a cat might do: take a nap in the morning, stretch out in the yard for a bit before lunch, nibble a bit of dry food here and there, find a dripping stream of water to lap at a for a while, hit the sack for an afternoon nap, and so goes the cycle. Now, I have met cats in fancy fluffy houses, and I have met cats that live on the street. I tell you they all enjoy life in about the same ways. I don't personally know Blackie or Tinker, but I can't think of anything they can do that I can't do, that I would have any interest in ever doing. Can you, my fellow kitties? Cats do not need. We just are. Humans can never be. They must strive, hunger, desire, and achieve. If any of you kitties get the idea in your head that you want to achieve like a human, just think about Blackie and Tinker. What more could you ever need than to simply just be a cat? And for you humans out there, for your own sake, try to learn from us cats, and just be.[2]

---

[2] Of course there are also dogs who have inherited giant sums of money, like Gunther, $145 million, and Trouble, $1.6 million inherited from Leona Helmsley (more than half of which was successfully stolen through lawsuits by ambitious, yearning human family members,) and it can be said that dogs also tend to prefer a simple life over material obsessions, but it is for entirely different reasons. Cats choose to live simply and shun materialism, while dogs are

And now, another piece of evidence of human stupidity: their computer software for writing is unable to grasp the concept of a footnote to a footnote, so instead of putting this footnote where I want to put it, I have to put it in the text. But it is a footnote to the last footnote and should go after "So, for their own sake, and those who have to clean up after them, don't give dogs money, okay humans?[3]

---

just too (what's a polite word for stupid?) to know the difference. If either of these "lucky" dogs were to have realized that he had the kind of purchasing power that he did, he probably would have spent it all on one huge, ginormous pile of human food, ate away at it for a continuous seventeen hours, until his stomach exploded and he died. So, for their own sake, and those who have to clean up after them, don't give dogs money, okay humans?

[3] Man, are dogs stupid. They don't even realize when they are full, so the humans have to cut them off before they eat themselves to death. If there is a stupider animal than one who would literally eat until his stomach exploded, I have yet to be introduced. Jesus, even ants know when to stop eating. Pathetic.

And once again, we must write this sentence in the regular page part to insert the next footnote, which was meant as a footnote to the other footnote. Why is the concept footnote to a footnote too hard for the human software??[4]

---

[4]Then of course, you have Gigoo the chicken ($10 Million), and Silverston the fifty-year-old tortoise ($27,000) who have also stumbled upon large amounts of human wealth. I don't really have much to say about chickens and tortoises except that if you keep chickens around the house, and let us hang around with the little baby ones, and we accidentally kill a couple, that is your fault not ours, and "tortoise" is really hard to spell. Humans and their ridiculous languages!

Chapter 20B
CATS SAVING HUMANS

I just wanted to take this brief moment to clear something up. There are a lot of stories out there about cats saving humans this way or that. They'll say this cat miraculously dialed 9-1-1 when its owner was in the process of dying or that the cat cried out from a room during a house fire, leading fire fighters right to the room where a human baby was trapped, or even more involved tales like this from the Huffington Post about a woman who had gone into a diabetic seizure:

> That's when Pudding sprang into action. The fast-acting feline sat on Jung's chest in an attempt to wake her up and when that didn't work, he nudged and nipped her face until she briefly returned to consciousness.
>
> In that moment, Jung was able to call out to her son Ethan, but he couldn't hear her calls. Luckily, Pudding darted into Ethan's room and pounced on the bed until he woke up and was able to call for help.

Not that I have a problem with taking credit where credit isn't due if that's your thing, but let's get serious here. Cats don't have time to save human lives. We are far too busy sleeping, eating, or . . . did I already say sleeping? We like you humans alright and everything, but we just can't be bothered by whatever situations you have gotten yourselves into by climbing up ladders (leave the climbing to us thanks) and eating ridiculous artery-clogging human foods. If we dial 9-1-1, it is probably because the phone happened to be where we wanted to be napping at that particular time, and as we flopped upon this phone, a couple numbers got dialed. Don't flatter yourself. If we are calling out to firefighters in the middle of a house fire, from the room where a sweet, little, innocent, baby human is goo-goo-ing and gaa-gaa-ing, it's because . . .WE ARE ALSO TRAPPED IN THE ROOM!! GET US OUT OF HERE!!!! And as for Pudding, who "sprung into action" to save Jung— come on now, "sprung into action?" Have you ever actually met a cat? Probably Jung's chest looked like a nice place to nap. But when she started seizing up, it started getting annoying, and she went over to see if there was any good sleep action to be had in Ethan's room, hence the description "pounced on the bed."

So, feel free to blog about your amazing cat stories, year after year, if it makes you feel good, but I think we all know the real deal here.

Chapter 21A
TROUBLESHOOTING CAT DOWNERS

Every so often, some external factor can be a bit of a downer. I mention the word external because given the right circumstances, a cat in an appropriate environment is pretty much flawless, and there should be no hardships to deal with. But the world is what it is, and sometimes other peoples' and animals' mistakes and flaws can intrude upon our otherwise peaceful, perfect existence.

Dealing with Jealousy

It is very common for other animals to be jealous of us cats because we are so obviously the most beautiful, charming, and wise of the animals. How does one deal with these jealousy issues? First, try not to care too much. Remember, this is not your problem, it is their problem. Second, sleep it off. If you are feeling bothered by the resentment other animals have towards you and your beauty and grace, take a nap, maybe you will feel better after some good rest. Finally, try to forget about it. In fact, I am already starting to forget about what the point of this chapter was.

Dealing with Things Getting Broken in the House

The humans have an unnatural attachment to material objects and have a hard time dealing with them getting disassembled. For example, they often keep very nice flowers in big heavy glass vases in various locations in the house. When we come by and get our faces all up in those flowers, sniffing, nibbling, rubbing whatever seems right at the moment, sometimes these vases subsequently become disassembled on the floor. This often causes a very loud noise, which can be disturbing even to a cat, let alone a nervous wreck of a human. Your human will probably start getting very upset when this happens and be ridden with guilt for making such a foolish mistake as to have put that nice vase in a place where it was so likely to fall. So what do you do in these situations? Try not to let it stress you, get a little sleep, and move on to some other things. Eventually, the human will get over their mistake, and buy a newer, bigger vase, which will also become disassembled on the floor during some good sniffing, and so the cycle of life continues. What can you really do—humans are imperfect beings!

Chapter 22
CAT PARENTING: DO'S AND DON'TS

Actually, I don't have any do's and don'ts. I just put that in because you have to if you want parents to read anything on the subject. What I have instead is Good News and Bad News.

Let's start with the Bad News: girls, you're not going to get any help from your kittens' father. He was long gone months before your litter arrived. At least with humans, the dads do some of the parenting, *in theory*. That's an important caveat that female humans don't always get. It's partly because they buy magazines with articles like, *Modern Dads Doing More Parenting than Their Fathers.* The reason these articles exist is to sell magazines. The follow-up article, designed to sell the next month's issue is: *Top Ten Tips on How to Get Your Husband to Do More Parenting.*

But there is one chore dads are expected to do: provide a role model for their male children. Unfortunately, the role model most dads understand they need to provide is that dads don't *do* much parenting. This lesson is passed on from generation to generation of men. But it's not *just* that. Another chore they have is driving the babysitter home. If they can do that without trying to *seduce* the babysitter, they've done a good job of role modeling, and they can be proud.

And now the Good News: there really isn't a lot of parenting that female cats are required to do. Once the litter is born, you clean them up a little, get them arranged at your teats, and they figure out nursing pretty quick. You purr a little while they're nursing, and they pick that up pretty quick also, and then you just lay back and relax.

After that, the only other thing you do is wean them, which you do when you're sick and tired of nursing, which will be pretty soon. Just hiss and snarl a little, if necessary attack them; they'll get the idea. Then your humans will palm them off on other humans, and you can go back to sleeping. Unfortunately, sometimes they can't palm all of them off, and you're stuck with a couple of them, which the humans are forced to keep—generally the least appealing of the litter—and you'll have to put up with them eating your food and sleeping where you need to sleep. Hopefully, your humans will then have you spayed, and you won't have to go through any of this ever again.

Chapter 23
CAT ALTRUISM

There is no such thing as Cat Altruism. Get over that right now.

Chapter 24
INSTINCT: HUNTING, KILLING, AND OTHER FUN STUFF

It's not like Sekhmet, Great Cat Goddess of Ancient Egypt, said, "Okay, we need some cat hunters and killers, also some cat farmers, and some cat intellectuals and academics. Let's start with the farmers. Volunteers? Why don't I see any paws raised?"

No, it didn't happen that way. There was no Committee of Cats that divided up responsibilities. "Who wants to be in charge of the Cat Farmers' Sub-Committee? Come on, girls, someone has to do this. It can't always be the same cats." That never happened for so many reasons.

1) Cats don't do committees.
2) Cats don't volunteer. We don't cooperate, we don't have co-ops, we don't have responsibilities; and if we did, we wouldn't divide them up.
3) We don't do democracy.

We don't do any kind of government, but if we did, it would be an absolute monarchy. There would be a queen (and that would be me), and the queen would issue commands, which could not be questioned or disobeyed. If you questioned, disobeyed, or even didn't move quickly enough to execute my commands, you would be ripped apart by my guards. Shredded. Thrown to the dogs. There would be no appeals of any kind, much less appeals for clemency.

We are all hunters and killers; nobody volunteered for it, it's just what we are. Turn your back on us at your own risk, friend.

Chapter 25
THE CONSCIENCE OF A CAT

As I understand it, the concept of "conscience" is a human construct, which goes something like this: "It could advance my self-interest to lie, cheat, or steal, but I won't do it, because it would be wrong." Or: "I have advanced my self-interest by lying, cheating, and stealing, but I feel badly about it."

With cats, the idea of a conscience is more like, "I got caught doing something I wasn't supposed to do, and I feel bad about being caught. Next time I won't get caught." Cats are more honest than humans. When a human is caught, normally the human apologizes—not for being caught, but for doing the bad thing.

Leadership

Leadership is apparently the goal of human education. Education is a punishment adult humans inflict on their children, because they can't take revenge on their own parents, who inflicted education on them, because their parents are too old.

Instead, they wreak it on their children. But even if this goal of developing the Leaders of Tomorrow was achieved (and it never is), there would be a big problem. If every human being becomes a leader as a result of their excellent education, who's left to become followers? There have to be a lot more followers than leaders, so if they were being honest, humans would have to admit that the goal of education is to provide the Followers of Tomorrow.

But really, I couldn't care less what humans do or don't do. If they want to punish their children with education, that's fine, as long as it doesn't interfere with them providing me with food I will eat (in other words, not that crap you just bought a lot of), my Minimum Basic Allotment of Petting, and a variety of excellent sleeping locations and rugs to puke on.

Chapter 26
THE INTERNATIONAL ASSOCIATION OF CATS

Rather than trying to explain the purpose of the International Association of Cats, I'm going to present the minutes of the last annual membership meeting, so you can see the organization in action.

Minutes of the Annual Membership Meeting, International Association of Cats

I'd like to welcome everybody to the annual membership meeting of the International Association of Cats. Once again, I see that nobody has shown up. I would read the minutes of last year's meeting, but nobody showed up for that one either, so there are no minutes to read. All items on this year's agenda are tabled indefinitely.

If any of the Chaircats of the various subcommittees would like to report on the work they have done since last year's meeting, I strongly advise that they attend the Annual

Membership Meeting so they can report. If you don't show up, you can't submit a report, can you? That is pretty obvious to me. I suppose you could send an email or something, but I haven't gotten any emails, so I think you don't have anything to report.

Also: I resign. I never wanted to be Chaircat in the first place. Since obviously there is no new business, and there wasn't any old business, I move and also second the movement to adjourn the meeting. The meeting is adjourned.

Chapter 26A
THE INTERNATIONAL CAT UNION

The International Cat Union, or ICU, is a union devoted to advancing the interests of cats. It is not to be confused with the Intensive Care Unit. That ICU is a waste of money which could be better spent on inexpensive vaccines for deadly diseases in Africa, where humans could save millions of lives if they cared to. But of course they don't. Never mind. I'm indifferent to the bad choices humans make.

But back to the cat union. It will be up to the membership to decide what issues are important enough to call a strike, and when a strike is called, exactly what that would mean. We could, for example, withhold all purring until we get what we want, or refuse to sit in human laps. This could be effective, but then we wouldn't get our Minimum Basic Allowance of Petting Time (the MBAP) of at least two hours. So it's problematic, but the membership needs to make sacrifices now and then to advance the interests of cats.

Any downgrading of cat food, for example, is a strike issue. It's already suspiciously filled with "extenders" and other meat and fish substitutes they put in. They could even be putting dog meat into it, which might be alright, but they should label it properly and not call it "Beefy Delight" when it really should be called "Doggie Delight." Just want to know what I'm eating, that's all.

There's one other issue that would make me support a strike, and that is the issue of introducing a dog into my house without first getting permission from me. I don't want to hear, "Look! We got a dog!" What I want to hear is, "We were thinking about getting a dog, but only if that's okay with you. If it isn't, of course we won't get one."

Chapter 27
CAT SPORTS

Here is an example of a sport that is not for cats: football. Why is football not for cats? Let's count the ways:

1) Eleven guys on offense. We don't do eleven cats on anything. Offense, defense, even just hanging out with ten other cats. No, thanks.
2) Equipment. We don't do equipment.
3) Coaches. We do not accept coaching.
4) Penalties. We do not serve penalties, nor do we accept penalties.

If you throw a brightly colored handkerchief down next to me, I will rip it to shreds.

Here is an example of a cat sport: curtain-surfing. It's a little like body-surfing in that it requires no special equipment, like a surfboard. With curtain-surfing you just bring what Sekhmet, cat goddess of ancient Egypt, gave you: your cat body, specifically, your claws. You leap off a nearby bookshelf, do a four-claw landing, on hopefully something delicate like lace, and ride the curtain all the way down to the bottom. It should make a very satisfying ripping sound.

Of course anything with string is a possible cat sporting event, and yarn especially, if it's being woven into a sweater, has cat sport written all over it.

Cats of good will have different opinions regarding the knocking over of glasses full of water or other liquids. Many cats regard this as entirely suitable for the Cat Olympics where the knocking over of the glass is evaluated by cat judges for both athletic and artistic merit. But others point to the infamous 1964 Cat Olympics in Barcelona, where the competition was marred by controversy. Siamese cat judges were accused of unfairly marking down the memorable performance of an American cat and giving a Siamese cat way higher marks than she deserved.

Also there was the blood doping scandal, as a result of which the Gold Medal in Mouse Throwing, awarded to American Mouse Thrower Herbert N. Cat was taken back. That is, it was officially taken back, Herbert never actually surrendered it. His record throw of 55.2 meters still stands, although not officially in the record books.

Below is a candid photo taken during the warm-ups for the Mouse Throwing event at the 1992 Mexico City Cat Olympics.

Note the intense concentration
of both cat and mouse as they
prepare for the first throw.

There is another sport, an indoor sport, which some cats enjoy: pool.

Eight ball, side pocket. Yes, I *did* call it.

Chapter 28
CAT THERAPY

"So Fiona, tell me about your dreams."

"Well, Dr. Kirby, I've been having this dream where I'm being chased by dogs, and then suddenly I'm in a car, going to the vet. When I get there, the vet is a sadist."

"All vets are sadists, Fiona."

"But I know this vet hates me. He hurts me on purpose."

"Who else has hurt you on purpose, Fiona?"

"Nobody. Except . . ."

"Except?"

"Well, my mother of course, when she was weaning me."

"Do you think the vet might have been your mother, Fiona?"

"The vet was my mother, Dr. Kirby? That's really preposterous. Surely you don't expect me to pay you for this nonsense, do you?"

Well, anyway, that's what a cat therapy session might sound like, if cats did therapy, but cats don't do therapy.

Chapter 29
CAT RELIGION

Cats don't do religion. We accept that humans have cat gods whom they worship, and we will accept worship, but we don't do any of it ourselves.

One of the big human religions, Catholicism, has this amusing process where the devout human believer does something he or she considers to be bad, then on Sunday goes to mass, and confesses the sin to a priest who sits behind a grate where you can't see him, and hears the confession. Then the priest gives them some prayers to say, after which they are forgiven for the sins.

Cats don't even apologize, much less confess. We are what we are, we do what we do. You don't like it? Tough, get over it. If humans were a little more assertive, a little more like cats, they wouldn't have the problems they do. But they think they should be good, and then of course they're not good, so they feel bad and give themselves a very hard time about it. Really pathetic.

Chapter 30
CAT ART

Cats do not do watercolors, oils, charcoal, abstract, or realistic sculptures, mobiles, or origami for one, very good reason: A cat *is* a work of art.

Humans like to take a perfectly acceptable wall and disrupt it with a painting. They will also take an acceptable mantel or bookshelf and mar it with a sculpture. There's not much we can do about the paintings, but we can jump up on a mantel or bookshelf and sweep the offending sculpture off of it, and with any luck it will smash into a thousand tiny pieces, and you can blame the whole thing on the dog.

Who but the dog could have done this? The dog probably did it, in fact, the dog *definitely* did it!

A cat is living, breathing, moving-around art. Not at all like a dog, which is a distraction, an annoyance, a disruption. Not like a human, which is all those bad things a dog is plus a lot of other bad things, including a source of unpleasant odors and pointless noise.

A cat brings peace and dignity to a room. A quiet sense of meaning, purpose, and beauty. What is art if not an attempt to give life meaning, purpose and beauty?

How to Feel about Art

Young kittens may be confused about art, so I will try to explain it to you. I do believe that we cats can be expressively artistic, clearly in different ways than humans. I believe, for example, that sleeping is an art. I feel I best express myself by and through sleeping. I have offered a few haikus in this book as well. You can feel free to explore different areas of art, but I wouldn't waste too much time on it. Humans, on the other hand, waste huge amounts of time on art. They are always painting this or singing that, dancing around in circles, or writing poetry, all in an attempt to express their inner souls and the woes, joys, and sorrows of being human. Most cats like to eat, sleep, chase mice—don't need to read Shakespeare to figure out that one.

Then, to make things worse, they also invest huge amounts of money in buying art, which just encourages the other humans to spend more time making it, instead of just napping through their problems, and so the cycle self-perpetuates. Cats don't make art for mass consumption in that way. We can be artistic as mentioned, but if we turned it into a product, who would buy it? Cats are really not interested in what other cats are doing or thinking, and we certainly don't care to hear about the longing and sorrows in their inner souls. Once again, better things to do.

Regarding human art, it will come as no surprise to you at this point that I am not impressed with most of it, in line with my lack of enthusiasm for most of the things humans do. If you must investigate for yourself, I will make a few recommendations of human artists and artwork worth reviewing. Cat Stevens is pretty good. The Stray Cats had a few good tunes, John Cougar Melencamp doesn't totally suck, and Def Leopard is listenable if you like that hair rock from the eighties. Most theater seems a waste of time to me, but, the musical "Cats" had some redeeming qualities. Don't care much for paintings either, but, "Sleeping Girl with Cat" by Pierre-Auguste Renoir is okay. "Woman with Cat" by Edouard Manet has a flowing, yet contrasting, vibrating and still earthy symmetry. "Wounded Bird with Cat" by Pablo Picasso is probably the greatest work of visual art ever made (by a human). Those are my picks, take 'em or leave 'em.

"As anyone who has ever been around a cat for any length of time well knows, cats have enormous patience with the limitations of the human kind."—Cleveland Amory

With all due respect to Cleveland, I disagree. It's not that we have patience, it's that we don't care.

Chapter 31
ANGER MANAGEMENT FOR CATS

This is a very simple concept. No cat therapist has ever led an Anger Management Class for cats for two good reasons: 1) There are no cat therapists, and 2) Cats don't have a problem with anger management.

Do we ever get angry? Of course we do! But we don't suppress that anger, we express it. If you keep the anger all bottled up inside, it can cause big problems. It can escape in a big, often inappropriate explosion directed against another human, dog, or even cat who happens to be in the wrong place at the wrong time. Or it can cause depression; at least that's the human therapists' line. Unexpressed anger is directed back at the source and becomes depression. Really can't comment on that one because we don't do either unexpressed anger or depression.

So this chapter is going to be very short, and if you don't like it, eat me. How about that? Does that kind of rude insult make you angry? Aw . . . Well, here's a couple of options for you: you can snarl and spit at this book, or you could stop reading altogether. Totally up to you. You've already bought the book, so I don't care.

Or maybe you're just leafing through it at the bookstore, so you haven't already bought it, which would be bad, but you're not really supposed to do that. You can look at the back jacket and the flaps, maybe even read a little from the beginning, but you can't just start reading Chapter 29. The Book Police will track you down and arrest you. Then you'll need a Cat Defense Lawyer, an interesting concept I might also write about at some point, but not now because I've already made this chapter too long.

Chapter 32
CAT MUSIC

Here's what a Cat Symphony Orchestra would look like: mostly stringed instruments, not too much in the way of brass or woodwinds. And the cat violinists and cellists would play mostly *pizzicato*, plucking the strings gently rather than drawing a bow across them, because we're uniquely gifted in *pizzicato*. When we're on tour in South America, it will be *pizzigato*, for our Spanish-speaking sisters.

The orchestra tunes up, an expectant murmur is heard from the packed house, and then the cat conductor takes her place, warmly applauded by the crowd. The orchestra begins to play an introduction, and then the cat soloists begin to sing. It's a beautiful blend of cat voices, a couple of tomcats singing bass and tenor, a soprano, and then me. I'm a mezzo soprano. The rich harmonies blend together as our voices soar out over the audience.

Except cats don't do any of that! We're *all* soloists and we don't sing solos together, we sing them separately. If there is more than one cat voice singing at the same time, you can be pretty sure it's part of a confrontation, and there's nothing harmonious about it. There is no blending, we don't keep the same tempo, and we *definitely* don't follow a conductor.

There's nothing more to be said.

The cat piano soloist makes her entrance.

Her virtuosity stuns the audience.

Tchaikovsky has never sounded as good.

These prodigies were co-winners of the Van Clyburn Prize in 2012.

The Brahms double concerto in E flat major.

Chapter 33
A TRIBUTE TO MICE

I like mice. Does this surprise you? It really shouldn't. For starters, they are really cute. Not like rats, which are not cute. Rats live in garbage-strewn back alleys, lurk in garages and attics, and spread disease. Remember the Black Plague? One-third of the entire population of Europe wiped out thanks to rats. Mice had nothing to do with that.

Besides cute, they are quick as a wink. There's no way a lazy cat is going to catch a mouse. Catching a mouse is a challenge, and also a good way for a cat to stay fit. Another thing: you can play with a mouse. If I catch one, I always bring it into the house, being very careful as I carry it in my mouth not to injure it. When I get it into the living room, I'll let it go, and of course it will scurry right under a couch. Then I watch and wait, staying very quiet and still. Eventually, the mouse will think I've gone away and will creep out from under the couch.

Then, it's Pounce Time! Nothing more thrilling for a cat than pouncing. I think the mouse enjoys this play, too. Maybe not quite as much as I do, but at least a little bit. Eventually, it will be time for one of my afternoon naps, so I'll let it go back outside, where it will scuttle back to its little mouse house. I think I will have contributed something to that mouse's appreciation of life because it probably thought when I caught it, that it was going to be The End. But now, it's living on borrowed time. Each day a new gift from God. Actually a gift from me. *Carpe diem*, little mouse!

There is also the fact that mice will leave little mouse poops right on the pillow of a nicely made human bed. It is pretty entertaining watching the humans when they discover this little gift. So many wonderful mouse behaviors, I'm sure I'm leaving something out. I really don't think they should use mice as guinea pigs for human medicine. You want a guinea pig? Use a guinea pig!

Some More Questions and Answers

Q: When is the best time to sleep?

A: That is an extraordinarily stupid question. Surely there's a kitten with a better question to ask.

Q: What kind of string is best to play with?

A: I'm not going to answer any questions that don't have at least a minimum amount of cat attitude in them.

Q: What gives you the right to tell us what to do?

A: Thank you! I can feel the hostility in that one! What gives me the right is that I'm an older, experienced cat, and you are a pathetic collection of the dumbest kittens I've ever encountered.

Q: Who made you so special?

A: Excellent question, dripping with contempt. Nobody made me special. I *am* special. And you are not. Well, I think I've squeezed about all the catlike attitude I can from you, so we'll be moving on to other subjects, not dependent on you asking good questions.

Words with "Cat" in Them

Catastrophe – This describes what happens when you leave things to humans and dogs to handle.

Catamaran – A kind of sailboat that is so much faster and more agile than all other sailboats that nobody races in anything but catamarans anymore.

Catapult – A device which can launch a dog from where the dog is now to maybe 150 yards away, which is a better location.

Cater – To attend to in a way that is so much better than merely "taking care of" that humans had to invent a different word for it, which is based on "cat."

Cattle – One cow, many cattle. The good thing about cattle is where there are cattle, there is usually a slaughterhouse not too far away, and when they go there, eventually there is cat food. Of course the humans take most of the good cuts first, but there's still enough good stuff that they can make decent cat food out of it, which you enjoy right up to the moment your human staggers into his house with a ton of it, which is when you change your brand preference. Now you hate that stuff, and won't eat it.

Not to wander too far afield, but these next cats have been given cat food by their humans, which they have found to be inadequate.

It is the unanimous ruling of this court that the cat food provided herein is completely unacceptable. Return immediately to the store and get something better.

Catatonic – State that humans wander around in most of the time. It's a bit like being in a coma, only they're awake. It would be less trouble if they were in a coma.

Cataract – Something that goes wrong with the human eye, so they can't see, and should be put to sleep.

Catcall – Loud or raucous cry made to express disapproval. Of course expressing disapproval is the only good reason for a loud or raucous cry.

Catch – Something you do to a prey animal, normally associated with fish, but really it can be any animal, or human.

Catch on – To become popular. 'Nuff said.

Categorical – Absolute. As in a categorical denial that it was me who puked on your stupid rug. It was the dog, obviously.

Catholicism – A very hierarchical human religion, where oddly, the head of it, the Pope, is not a cat, although the word "cat" is right at the beginning of the word. Somebody was not paying attention.

Cat-o'-nine-tails – A whip that humans used in the good old days for punishment which drew blood immediately. Don't get why they stopped using it, as it was very effective.

Catwalk – A narrow walkway overlooking a prison or an area where workers are working so you can see if they're working hard enough. Or behaving themselves in ways

This should clearly be a cat. A cat should be made available as a suitable object for veneration, if not outright worship.

acceptable to cats. Of course it is elevated, and of course you look down upon every creature below you.

Category – A group of things which is different from another one, like stupid dogs, incredibly stupid and annoying dogs, and dogs who are *unbelievably* stupid and annoying. Those are three different categories of dogs.

Cat house – A house of prostitution. Don't really get the connection.

Dog house – A metaphorical place where a human is put when he has done something very bad. Typically it's a male human who is in the dog house. He's done something like stay out too late, drink with the boys, and tried, unsuccessfully, to sneak back in, hoping his wife had gone to bed. Naturally, the worst place a human can imagine is a place where a dog would live. That much is true.

Catfight – Particularly nasty fight among two female humans. Well, they got one thing right: If it's a catfight, it's going to be particularly nasty.

Dogfight – This refers, oddly enough, to battles between war planes that humans have in their constant wars. I don't understand what aerial combat has to do with dogs. Dogs are so terminally innocent, that offered the chance, they would love to accompany a human into the sky in some kind of very dangerous warfare, because dogs always want to come along for a ride and never think that it might be their last one.

Catty – Slyly spiteful or malicious. Yup, that's us.

Cat Haikus

Wanting to eat food,
Begging, hoping, focusing.
The life of a dog.

The road less traveled
Still proceeds only to death.
Got any catnip?

Gaze not from your plate,
To yearn yields only more want,
And I'll eat your food.

Hey, are you working?
But I want to go outside.
I won't be ignored.

Having fun are we?
I never break a promise.
You shall rue this day

Humbly I warn thee,
My worthy adversary:
We shall meet again.

Intolerable.
A declaration of war.
I will bury you.

How was your trip, friend?
I've left a message for you:
Puke on your pillow.

Look! I've caught a bird!
Only feathers on a string.
Who me? I knew that.

That was on purpose.
I did not slip, how dare you?
I meant to do that.

Chapter 34
THE CAT DEFENSE LAWYER

If you were paying attention (not likely), you will recall that a little earlier I spoke of cat lawyers, but said I wouldn't be writing about them. Well, I've changed my mind. The best way to illustrate what a good cat defense lawyer is like is to imagine ourselves in a courtroom, where a cat has been accused of a crime, the evidence being a video taken by a surveillance camera, which seems to the unprofessional eye to be pretty good evidence. But here is what the cat defense lawyer says in her summation to the jury:

Cats of the jury: Let me begin by reminding you that under the law, a cat is innocent until she is proven guilty. Therefore, my client, as she sits before you now, is innocent. Why then, is she accused of the crime of sweeping a priceless vase off a high bookshelf, causing it to fall onto the floor into a thousand pieces? Because the prosecuting attorney wants to pad her résumé for a future run for political office! She wants to appeal to the law-and-order voters by boasting of all the cats she has sent to the pound! Does she know that my client is innocent? Probably. Does she care? No!

So let us look at the so-called "evidence." The video shows us only a brief shot of a cat, who happens to resemble my client but is *not* my client, jumping onto the shelf, sweeping the vase off the shelf, and then jumping down. If the cat who did this had been a black cat and my client also a black cat of approximately the same age and size, this case would not have been brought. But because my client is a black, white, gray, and brown tabby, a very common coloring, she has been wrongly accused.

Yes, the vase was broken, and yes a cat who *resembles* my client committed the vandalism. But why was my client wrongly accused? Because she was available! Because she was the house cat *nearest* to the crime, *not* because she actually committed the crime!

What did, in fact, occur? What did the "evidence" omit? Here is what happened: a cat (a well-known neighborhood stray), took advantage of an open window to enter the house. She then quickly ran into the living room, climbed up on the easy chair next to the bookshelf, and from there jumped onto the shelf, sweeping away the vase, and then retreated exactly the same way she had entered: shelf to chair, across the living room to the open window and out!

Members of the jury, I ask you to consider what may have happened, and what may have happened *beyond a reasonable doubt*. When you consider that, I am confident you will find the accused *not guilty!*

I am totally persuaded by the brilliant cat defense lawyer. I will vote to acquit. There could be a dog on the panel who will not consider the evidence, only vote against the cat no matter what. But if there is any justice, this cat will walk.

Here is a possible dog juror who would ignore the evidence and vote to find the cat guilty just because she's a cat:

This dog doesn't care about the evidence, it is totally biased against cats and should never have been allowed on the jury, but all the defense pre-emptories had been used up, and the judge, who could also have had this dog thrown off, is also biased against cats.

Chapter 35
BUSHES AND TREES: EXCELLENT FOR LURKING

There are hardly any better places for lurking than bushes and trees. They share the outstanding feature that you can lurk pretty much unseen in either. However, each has some disadvantages as well. If you're lurking in a bush, you should be invisible, and you certainly will be to humans. A dog, however, has a keen sense of smell. It would be a lot better for everybody if they didn't have such good smelling abilities. Even for humans it's bad because they can smell food from miles away, and they're going to be all over it, begging, whimpering, if possible stealing, and being very annoying.

But this smelling thing also means that while a dog won't see you lurking in a bush, it could possibly smell you lurking. And a bush is close to the ground, so dogs have access.

A tree, on the other hand, is inaccessible to a dog. Even if a dog smells you up there, there's not a damn thing he can do about it. Another good thing about a tree is that climbing it is a thrilling experience, and a great workout for your claws. However, once you're up there, queen of all you survey, there's the problem of getting back down. There don't seem to be any good ways for a cat to get *down* from a tree. At least if there is a good way, I haven't heard about it. So there's a pretty big *caveat*. Up: yes, down: not so much.

I don't like doing it, which is great because I almost never have to, but, every once in a while, I have to admit that there are a couple things not completely, 100 percent perfect about us cats. One of these things is that the curvature of our claws is perfectly, excellently designed for climbing up trees, but totally not useful at all for climbing back down. This is why from time to time you see one of our brothers or sisters pathetically whimpering for a human's help up on a branch of a tree. What usually happens, is one way or another, the cat makes it safely back down to the ground, and the human who has climbed up into the tree to retrieve the cat ends up with a broken leg.

So, really more for the sake of your humans than your own, just don't go there. I know it looks like a fun trip up, but try to think a little bit down the road, and realize that what goes up must come down.

Chapter 36
THE RULES FOR CATS

I'm just guessing, but I think this cat has not yet confronted the down problem.

ittens, listen up. You want to grow up to be responsible members of the cat community, so you have to know the rules.

There are no rules.

Cats don't do rules. Rules are for humans and dogs. Human rules are things like, Thou Shalt Not Commit Adultery, and Keep Off the Grass. Also, No Spitting, No Littering, and No Smoking. Dogs are eager to learn the rules, but of course they are way too slow to learn anything, much less something as complicated as Keep Off the Grass. You often see the following scene: A human with a dog on a leash at an intersection, instructing the dog sternly to sit. Then, after looking both ways for cars, the human gives the dog the okay to walk across the street. I suppose the human believes that if she does this a couple of thousand times, the dog will eventually learn to look both ways for cars before charging across the street, chasing after something important like a ball. This will never happen. The dog has no idea why it's supposed to sit, then walk across the street. Not a clue.

Cats don't need to worry about this because with the exception of tomcats, cats don't cross streets. The only thing worth chasing is a mouse, and mice don't cross streets, they scurry under houses. So if there's any chasing to be done, it's all around the house.

The other rules, all the "don'ts" and "it is forbidden to's," do not apply to cats. If they did, we certainly would pay no attention to them. Here's a good one: "No sleeping in the park." Really? You're going to tell me where I can sleep, human? Ha. Ha. Ha.

Chapter 37
CAT INTELLIGENCE

As a general rule, cats don't submit to testing. However, if there are some cats reading this book who'd like to know how smart they are, I will provide the following Cat IQ Test:

1) If 4 dogs are joined by another 8 dogs, and they all go chasing after a ball which bounces into the street, and a big truck comes along and runs over 7 of them, how many dogs are left?

   A) 15

   B) 5

   C) 7

   D) Too many

2) If you have visited your kitty litter 3 times to poop and 6 times to pee, and your humans still haven't cleaned it up yet, how many times have you visited your litter?

   A) 4

   B) 12

   C) 9

D) Enough times to leave a reminder message on the living room carpet

3) If your day has begun with a morning nap of a 1½ hours, to which you then added a second nap of 2 hours, and then an afternoon nap of 3 hours, and a nighttime 3½ hours, how many hours have you slept so far?

A) 5 hours

B) 9 hours

C) 12 hours

D) Not enough hours

Well, I think this test was too easy, but I have better things to do than make up harder questions. If you missed any of them, you should be able to commit a crime and then plead that your cat IQ is too low to be prosecuted like a normal cat.

Getting Into the Cat College of Your Choice

Fiona is escorted into the office of the Dean of Admission at the prestigious Cat University of North Carolina:

Dean Crumpet: Please have a seat, Fiona. Well, I see you prefer lying on the floor. Fine. You chose not to submit any scores from standardized tests. May I ask why?

Fiona: I don't do tests.

Dean Crumpet: That could be a problem, because we give them.

Fiona: You can give them. I don't take them.

Dean Crumpet: Well, perhaps we can work around that. You understand that we offer courses in valuable, practical aspects of cat life as well as the more academic stuff. For example, we have a course in Catching Mice.

Fiona: I know how to catch a mouse.

Dean Crumpet: You might be surprised by the fact that there are some tricks to catching mice you may not know about.

Fiona: I know how to catch a mouse.

Dean Crumpet: We're also very excited to have a visiting professor next semester who comes to us all the way from Africa, a leopard, who is going to share her expertise in chasing and bringing down a gazelle.

Fiona: I'm not going to be chasing and bringing down any gazelles.

Dean Crumpet: This professor will also teach you how to chase and bring down a human.

Fiona: I'm not going to be doing that either, not that I wouldn't like to.

Dean Crumpet: It's not about size, Fiona. It's about speed, the element of surprise, and knowing the exact location of the jugular vein.

Fiona: Well, I *might* be interested in that one.

Dean Crumpet: I'd suggest you sign up for that class today. It's filling up very fast.

Chapter 38
CUTE CAT VIDEOS WE WON'T BE MENTIONING IN THIS BOOK

This could be one of my favorite chapters, since it's all about stuff we won't be mentioning, so it's going to be really short, and then both author and reader can take a well-deserved nap.

For unimaginable reasons, humans think it's hilarious to dangle some enticing bit of fluff or food on the end of a string, just out of reach of a cat, and when the cat, responding to catch-and-kill instincts deeply embedded in her DNA, jumps up and tries to grab the item, the human snatches it away. They tape endless hours of this activity and post them on YouTube.

Not only is this not cute, it borders on something that could be presented in court on an abuse-of-authority case, or a war crimes trial. I confess I fell for this once or twice when I was a kitten, but I wised up a long, long time ago, so don't bother to even try this on me. I will puke on your pillow.

Since there's nothing more to be said here, you are excused, and I am excused. You can do whatever you want. I'm taking a long nap.

A Note on Water

Humans like to get useless products at pet stores. One of them is an expensive water dish with special pumps circulating and filtering the water. These are completely unacceptable. Water must be fresh, cold, and provided by humans on demand. Actually, the best water is the water the humans are drinking from their own glasses. You know that water will be cold and fresh, so just jump up on the table and go for it.

One other good kind of water is the water they put cut flowers in. You can usually access this water by sticking your head into the vase, but when this isn't possible or it's too much trouble, simply knock the vase over. The water will spill out on the table, and you can lick it up from there. This is also best done when the humans aren't around, and maybe they will blame the dog, which you should encourage. If there is no dog to blame, just disappear for a while so the humans will have time to adjust to the broken vase and spilled water. Eventually, they will realize there are more important things in their lives. They say, "If you've got your health . . ." In this case, if you've got your health, what's a broken vase and some water spilled on the table? They need to get over that, and just clean it up. This should give them a sense of accomplishment when they're done, something often lacking in their lives. So if you look at it a certain way, you've done them a favor.

Now that I think more deeply about this subject, I've decided it deserves it's own chapter. Therefore . . .

Chapter 39
A WHOLE CHAPTER ON WATER (AS OPPOSED TO THE NOTE)

Humans and dogs are quite a bit behind cats in evolutionary advancement. Not so long ago, dogs and humans crawled out of the oceans and evolved things like legs, noses, and a strange fascination with Frisbees. Cats, however, are much further along in our evolution, and it has been a lot longer since we lived in the water. This is part of why we do not like water, at least when it comes to being physically immersed in a body of it. When humans and dogs paddle around in rivers and pools, or hose off in a shower or rainstorm, it reminds them of their days as little fishies joyfully exploring pre-Triassic Earth. When we are forced into a water situation, it just reminds us of how much we hate water. So, if it occurs to you that maybe you want to jump into the pool and paddle around like the dopey dogs, just a forewarning that you will not enjoy it, so, don't go there.

We do, however, like water when it comes to the act of drinking. Water is quite enjoyable for consumption, while being completely annoying for bathing. But, there is good water for drinking, and then there is much better water for drinking. Good water for drinking is any body of water that has been assigned to us as "our water." This usually comes in a colored bowl-type vessel, as shown below. Don't get me wrong, the water assigned to us as "our water" is all well and good and I encourage you to drink it from time to time. It's easy and it's always there. But, there is much better water available.

One example of a better water source is a faucet. Although there may not be a steady stream of water, there is from time

to time a periodic drip, which makes this water all the more tantalizing. It is important to locate all of the different faucets you have access to, and identify which ones are currently producing goods.

Another better source of water is a human's glass of water, (seen here).

It is more enjoyable to drink this water as it tends to be a bit colder than "our water." There is the added pleasure of knowing that we aren't really supposed to be drinking it, and we frequently get chased away in the process. Unfortunately for the humans, they have so many, many things on their minds and tasks to take care of that they find it very difficult to defend their glass of water in a comprehensive fashion. We, however, have nothing to do except vigilantly wait for that sweet moment when the human has moved away from the glass of cool refreshing water, and we are left alone with our helpless prey. At times, it can be tricky to get to the water, as it may be a half drunken glass we are dealing with. Be wary! If you stick your face too far into the glass, you may get stuck! A far better way of dealing with this is to use your paw to dab at the water, and lick it. This is an efficient and reliable method, but you do run the risk of knocking the glass over. This is something the humans don't like. However, it is not something you should be too concerned about. Someone else will clean this up. You can continue going about your daily activities.

The best source of water is the unexpected discovery. Maybe a hose in the backyard has begun to leak a bit, leaving a little puddle. Maybe on the roof there is a little pool of water from last week's rainstorm still lingering around. These are your most excellent sources of water; they are just yours for your memories, as they may never be seen again. Enjoy these Zen moments and feel free to write in with your favorite finds!

Even More Questions and Answers

Q: What is the origin and meaning of "raining cats and dogs"?

A: I have no idea. I could imagine what the meaning of the phrase "raining dogs" might be: it would be a way of describing an unmitigated catastrophe, a nightmare so horrible that it would wake me from my mid-afternoon nap.

Q: What's the origin and meaning of "cat got your tongue"?

A: Again, I have to admit I don't know. I certainly don't want your tongue, and wouldn't know what to do with it if I had it.

Q: The "cat's pajamas"?

A: I don't do pajamas, and I've never heard of any cat who wears them, or has anything to do with them. However, according to Urban Dictionary, it was a popular phrase used by hipsters in the 1920s to describe a person who is best at what they do. This doesn't surprise me at all, it's logical enough. If there was also a phrase, "the dog's pajamas," that would be used to describe a person who is the worst at what they do.

Q: What about, "sitting in the catbird seat"?

A: This means on top of your game, on top of the world, being at the right place, at the right time, the best seat in the house. I'm thinking that maybe the bird comes into it because the cat has just eaten the bird, so the cat is now sitting where the bird was previously sitting.

Q: "Catnap"?

A: A catnap is a nap of short duration, because a dog or a human has needlessly interrupted a cat who would have napped for a much longer time.

Q: "The cat's meow"?

A: Another phrase that means the very best of something. There really should be a prize named after this phrase, The Cat's Meow Prize, which would be way better than the Nobel or the Pulitzer prize.

Q: What is a "cat person"?

A: When a human asks another human if she has a dog, the other human says, "No, I'm more of a cat person." What they should say is, "A dog? Why would I have a dog? That's absurd! I have a cat, of course. Everybody should have a cat. Just one is best, but if absolutely necessary, you can have two."

Q: Caterwaul?

A: Human dictionary definition: to make a harsh cry, to quarrel noisily. All this really means is when you hear it, you better pay attention. You better pay attention whenever you're being addressed by a cat, of course, but especially in response to cater-wauling.

Q: Catholic?

A: Human religion that has nothing to do with cats. The word starts out with promise, but what follows is a huge disappointment. Cats are not worshipped by Catholics, there are no stained glass windows in their cathedrals depicting cat gods, it's all a lot of mumbo-jumbo, wholly lacking in cats.

Q: Is it ever cute to dress up a cat in human clothes and take a photo of it?

A: That is never cute. Let us consider the following not-cute photo:

Would you like to know what I think of the bow-tie thing? Take a look on your pillow when you go to bed tonight. Also in your shoes.

Another cat with something on her mind:

Do you think putting this blanket around me and taking a photo of it is cute? Is that what you think, human? Check your pillow tonight for my personal response.

Q: Do tigers have a good sense of hearing?

A: No, their hearing is not good. This next tiger is having trouble understanding a question:

Excuse me, I didn't hear you, would you mind coming a little closer so I could understand you better? Closer than that. Yeah, a little closer, please.

Q: Which animal is superior as a guard, a dog or a cat?

A: The same animal who is superior at everything. Here is an example of a guard cat, who is clearly on the job, as opposed to being easily distracted by food, normally used by burglars to distract a dog.

Yeah, I am watching you. Definitely and completely. I am all over you, buddy.

Here is another cat—not a guard cat, but a spy cat. She is disguised as a feather duster. The dogs, who are plotting to overthrow the government, think they are unobserved, but as they are all the time, they are wrong.

My superiors at the Cat Intelligence Agency will be very interested in what I am overhearing because these stupid dogs think I'm a feather duster. Tomorrow I'll return, disguised as a fluffy pair of slippers.

Q: Is there such a thing as a funny-looking cat?

A: Let's have a look at the following photo:

Now, *you* tell *me*: funny-looking or not funny-looking?

Chapter 39A
HELPING OUT AROUND THE HOUSE

Humans are always trying to do things faster. The reason for this is . . . well, I don't know what the reason is. Maybe they want to move on from doing something they know how to do, like painting the living room, to something they don't know how to do, like fixing their computer. Whatever the reason, they're always thinking up new time-saving devices. For example, for thousands of years they used paint brushes to paint things, then sometime in the last century, some human genius came up with the roller. That meant instead of dipping a brush into a can of paint, they poured the paint out into this roller pan, then rolled the roller in the paint and slapped it onto the wall.

Since they're so interested in speed painting, we can help out by jumping into the roller pan with the paint and then running around on the floor, or even better, on an expensive carpet. The aesthetic enhancement we can make to a regular floor or expensive carpet by adding a trail of bright blue cat paws to it is simply huge. It's a wonder that humans don't seem to appreciate it, but then they don't know much about art.

Or music. A cat can make an otherwise ordinary piano piece really rock by jumping onto the keys and playing alongside a human. There should be a lot of music written for human and cat. There would be an introduction for just the human, and then along about, say, measure forty there would be a Cat Entrance. But cats don't really follow musical scores, it has to be more spontaneous. When we feel the time is perfect, we jump up onto the keys and play. More like jazz than classical. It's all about feeling and improvisation.

Chapter 40
CAT PHILOSOPHY

Human philosophers have worked themselves into quite a panic over the centuries trying to answer the question, "Why am I here?" Another good one is, "What is the meaning of life?" Also, "How do I know the world is real, and not just a figment of my imagination?"

Let's take a look at these questions from the perspective of a cat philosopher. Starting with the last one, "How do I know the world is real and not just a figment of my imagination?" That is such an incredibly irrelevant question, it is not worth a response of any kind. The first two, "Why am I here?" and "What is the meaning of life?" are really just different ways of posing the same question. The answer is, "You are here, human, to provide your cat with acceptable cat food (not the cat food you just bought) and a variety of acceptable Sleep Locations, which must be kept clear of other objects, and especially dogs. You are also here to provide your cat with not less than two hours of daily petting." You see how simple it is to answer these questions?

There is dog philosophy too, which is not quite as lame as human philosophy, but almost as lame. A dog philosopher asks himself, "How can I get more food right now, and if I can get more food now, how can I get even more later?" Not very deep, but there's a certain focus there.

A cat philosopher asks the question, "Can you leave me alone so I can sleep?" "Can you get rid of the dog?" "Why are you talking?" "Why are you making noise of any kind?" "Why don't you take the dog out to the park and stay there for the next four hours?"

Chapter 41
FACECAT

Welcome to my Facecat page. If there are any cats reading this who are not on my friends list at the moment but would like to be: don't ask me to add your name, I'm not accepting any more friends.

In fact, if you're already on my friends list, I'd prefer if you removed yourself from it. Why? Here is why: If I happened to be asleep, (which I am most of the time) and you snuck into my house, you would eat my food. I don't want you to eat my food. I hear you saying, "But Cleopatra, I *wouldn't* eat your food, I'm your friend!" Really? I would eat *your* food, if I got the chance. I'm not sure I want you as a friend if you aren't the kind of cat who would *eat my* food.

So this is problematic. If you would eat my food, I don't want you as my friend, but if you would *not* eat my food, I *also* don't want you as my a friend.

The solution might be for me to cancel my Facecat page, but I *do* like to post my opinions about things, and also pointless accounts of my daily activities. You can read them, if you like, but I don't want to read yours, and I *definitely* don't want to be reminded about your birthday. I don't care about your birthday, and I don't particularly want to hear from you on *my* birthday. I just want to take a nap, and so that's what I'm going to do right now.

Chapter 42
BONDING WITH YOUR HUMANS

It may surprise you to hear me speak of the importance of bonding with your humans. In fact, it *should* surprise you, and if it does not, it means you haven't been paying attention, or you have the intelligence of a dog. But bonding with your humans is important. Not for sentimental reasons, but for what can best be described as business reasons.

The bonding I'm speaking of is not at all like the bond that forms between a human and a dog. A dog is mindlessly devoted to its human. A dog believes his human makes the sun come up in the morning. Every time the human makes a move for the front door, the dog is sure that he is welcome to come along, and the human is most likely going to the park to throw a stick or a ball for the dog to retrieve, a completely inane activity which dogs love.

No, we're talking about the importance of training whichever human has adopted you, because you are such a cute kitten. Pretty soon, you will be a cat, and not as cute. It will be difficult to find another human to adopt you, and much harder to train one. You need to "bond" with your human so it will understand exactly how to pet you, when you want petting and when you don't, which cat food brand is your current favorite, and which sleeping locations are yours, not theirs.

When your human takes a trip to go someplace else for some reason, usually "business" or "pleasure," you'll be left with a cat sitter, who will have to be trained. This takes a while, and probably won't be finished until your human suddenly reappears, and the whole cat sitter training will have been a waste of time.

At least you can be sure that sooner or later your human will return. Dogs, while they worship their humans, are thrown into a state of absolute panic when their humans go off on a trip, convinced that their humans have abandoned them. It doesn't make a lot of sense: The human/god is going to abandon its dog? Of course it's no concern of ours, unless we happen to have the misfortune of living with a dog, who will be so stressed during the human's absence that our entire nap schedule will be disrupted.

The cat-human bonding thing is more like a business arrangement. Just remember that. And remember also that you are in control of this relationship, not them. If you can remember these things, I recommend forging a bond with your human. If you can't, then don't bother.

Another Q & A

Q: Why are there so many short chapters in this book?

A: We spend sixteen hours of every day sleeping. Only eight hours awake. Do the math. Not enough time for long chapters.

Q: Is not being awake long enough every day the only reason there are so many short chapters in this book?

A: It's the most important reason. Also, when I cover a subject, I do it thoroughly but quickly. If you want long chapters, read a book written by a human.

Q: Humans write long chapters because they are awake too long every day?

A: Exactly. They can't fall asleep because they worry too much about stupid things, so they get out of bed, then take a reasonably-sized chapter and make it way too long.

Q: They do this because they can't fall asleep?

A: That is why they do that today. At one time, humans were paid for their writing by the word. So naturally they went on and on. The famous human writer on the next page, for example, was paid by the word.

Q: Russians wrote the longest books?

A: There was an Irish guy, James Joyce, who wrote really long books, but the Irish have a problem with not ever knowing when to stop talking, not to mention drinking, so maybe he wasn't paid by the word, maybe he was just, you know, Irish.

Charles Dickens, famous human writer, shown here thinking how he could pad his latest chapter so he could get paid more. I'm sure the guy who wrote *War and Peace,* Leo Tolstoy, was also paid by the word. Maybe the only novel that was longer than *War and Peace* was *Anna Karenina,* also by this dude. If I had to find another title for the book you are reading now, it would be: *Not War and Peace.*

Q: Can I ask another question?

A: No, I'm getting sleepy now. Go and nap, and I will also go and nap.

Chapter 43
BEST SUPPORTING CAT OSCAR

Let's be clear: cats don't support anybody. I certainly don't, so I'm not accepting any awards for Best Performance in a Supporting Role I would, however, accept an award for Best Cat Actress. Because I know there's a lot of interest, here's my acceptance speech:

> Thanks for this, I totally deserve it. Honestly, there was no competition, it was a foregone conclusion, any fool would have given it to me. I'd thank my agent, the studio executives who believed in me, and my family—my tomcats, and all my kittens—except for the fact that their support had nothing to do with me winning this award. I won it on my own, by myself. There isn't much more to say, but know this: If you want me to star in your next lousy film, it's going to cost you big time. And you'll be dealing directly with me since I'm firing my agent. All she ever did was hold me back, and collect 10 percent. That is over as of this moment.

Chapter 44
RUBBING UP AGAINST THINGS

One of the most important things you must do many times per day is rub up against a variety of different objects. You have to make sure that you reserve time in your schedule for doing this, and if this means taking time away from other activities, then so be it. This is not something you can put aside; it must be one of your top priorities.

I will proceed to give you some guidelines on how to go about doing this properly. Most of the rubbing will occur around the cheek and ear area, but there are also appropriate times for body rubbing. I will start with cheek and ear. Most objects can be used to target these areas, but certain objects are better than others. Pointy, hard objects will be especially useful. What you want to do is the line up the pointy object right around the crack of where your mouth ends and your cheek begins. Now, really smush your face in to the object, in a semi-circle fashion towards the ears. This will be your standard, go-to motion for cheek smushing.

In the following illustration, you see a cat that is attempting this with an object that is clearly too soft. Okay, it will work in some cases, but, let's not start developing bad habits here.

In this illustration, our subject has found a hard, rocky surface and is attempting to get some good ear smushing going on in a downward, circular motion. This is also going to work for you sometimes, but do you see the amount of contorting and twisting of the neck she is going through to pull this off? It is once again, not an ideal object for cheek smushing.

This final cat however, has found a much more suitable object. The little wooden chair has protruding corners that are hard and accessible at eye level. Once this cat determines which of the corners is best, he is in for a real cheek-smushing treat.

Regarding rubbing with other parts of the body: the most important of these techniques is scratching the back. Yes, you can brush up against a sofa and rub your sides against a human leg, but these are not as thoroughly enjoyable as a good back scratch. The best is a rough, hard surface on the floor. In the following illustration you see this cat has found an outstanding, rough stony surface and is taking full advantage. Notice how he is rolling from one side to another.

Your job today is to go around and try to identify the best objects and surfaces for both cheek smashing and back scratching. Even when you have identified some personal favorites, you should never close your mind to new surfaces and objects. Keep exploring and your life will be full of new surprises.

Chapter 45
CAT MYTHS

There are a handful of myths about cats that I would like to clear up once and for all.

First, we are not interested in "getting" anyone's tongue.

It would be a foolish mouse who plays when we are away, because we will be able to smell where it is and get a better idea of how to catch it next time, so, just not true.

I don't care how much room you think you have in your house, you swing one of us around and you will pay for it, one way or another.

Cats do not swallow canaries. We may catch one or two, but swallow? Only occasionally, as covered elsewhere in this book.

Cats cannot be herded, this one is true.

A cat would never put herself on a hot tin roof to begin with.

Yes, in general you should let sleeping cats lie, but if you have something to offer like a good petting (more than three-minutes' worth), it is okay to wake a cat, we don't really mind. That said, you should always let a sleeping dog lie. So much better than an awake dog, though not as good as a non-existent dog.

While it is hard to prove the historical accuracy that it was in fact curiosity that killed the cat, I would contend it was much more likely that the curious cat was totally in control of the situation until some bumbly, awkward human bumped into her and screwed up the whole thing.

We don't have nine lives. (See Chapter 21 for a more in-depth discussion.)

Black cats are not bad luck.

Cats don't wear pajamas.

I hope that clears up some of the lingering doubts out there.

Cats are arrogant. Truth: Cats are far too perfect creatures to have downsides like arrogance.

Chapter 46
CAT DANCING

As previously discussed, cats are natural musicians, and our instrument is the piano. We can definitely tickle the ivories.

But dancing is more problematic. For example, until the 1960s, dancing normally required two humans, moving together, usually touching or holding on to each other. We don't do that. The only kind of dancing we might consider is solo dancing.

Fortunately, sometime during the late 50s or 60s, humans let go of the together type of dancing, in favor of solo dancing where they would kind of jump around spastically in front of each other. So in theory they were still dancing "with" one another, but not really. That, we could do. But it begs the question, "Why?" Why would we want to prance around in front of another cat? It's difficult enough to have to share space with another cat, so why jump around like a an idiot? Even dogs don't dance. Wolves supposedly dance, or at least the humans made a bad movie at one time called, *Dances With Wolves*. I'm not sure if there were any wolves dancing in it, but that was what it was called.

But *Dances With Wolves* is a bit of a digression from our topic, which is cat dancing. The only thing I've ever seen that looks remotely similar to cat dancing are these awful YouTube videos where they manipulate a few moments of a cat walking across a room and make it go backwards and forwards. Humans think that is very clever, sometimes they even add a soundtrack to it. Ha, ha. I am not amused.

It looks like, once again, we've exhausted a subject. But once again, the good news is that I can take another nap, and you can do whatever you want to do. Whatever floats your boat, pal. Just don't tell me about it, I don't want to know.

Chapter 47
THE CAT BILL OF RIGHTS

1. Freedom to yowl.
2. Freedom to sleep.
3. Freedom to nap.
4. Freedom of non-association.
5. Freedom to be left alone.
6. Freedom from unreasonable dogs.

7. Freedom to sharpen our claws on whatever we want to sharpen them, whenever we feel like doing that.

8. Did I mention freedom to nap?

9. Freedom from pointless YouTube cat videos.

10. Freedom from veterinarians.

Chapter 48
THE TEN COMMANDMENTS OF SEKHMET

1. I am the Lord thy God, thou shalt have no others. Period. Get rid of them, right now, smash their statues, throw out the pieces.
2. Thou shalt not kill me. You can kill each other if you like. Just not me.

3. Thou shalt not steal my food or Excellent Sleeping Locations.

4. Thou shalt never disturb my nap.

5. Thou shalt feed me when I'm hungry.

6. Thou shalt keep my litter clean and change it regularly.

7. That cat food thou hast been feeding me? I don't like it anymore. Get rid of it.

8. The litter thou hast just bought? Won't use it. Get another brand.

9. Get rid of the dog.

10. I am bored with this now. Write thine own Tenth Commandment.

I'll Take a Few More Questions

Q: Why do we need so much more sleep than humans?

A: Humans have no natural ability for extended sleeping. It's partly because they're so busy doing whatever it is they do, they don't have time for it.

Q: Are there any other reasons?

A: While they have large heads and large brains, most of their brain cells don't function. They're just dead weight. Our smaller brains are fully functional, so we require more time to rest these brain cells from our waking activity.

Q: What *do* humans do?

A: Who knows? They normally go off to "work" or "school" in the morning, and do whatever it is to do there. When they get home they spend their evenings complaining about it to each other.

Q: Then why do they *go* to work or to school?

A: It's better not to spend too much time wondering why humans do what they do.

Q: What about dogs? They also sleep more than humans, but not as much as we do.

A: While it's probably not a good idea to spend too much time wondering about humans, it's *definitely* not a good idea to spend time wondering about dogs.

Q: But why do dogs sleep on couches and comfy chairs?

A: You ask that question as though there was some logic behind why dogs do what dogs do. Their only logic is food. If a dog thinks that something he could do might end up getting him some food, he will do it. Barking, whimpering, wagging his tail, looking longingly at the food, jumping, running in circles, whatever. Other than that there is no logic to dog behavior. Just thinking about dogs has made me tired and a little grumpy. Nap time!

A Couple More Haikus

Priceless antique vase
Sorry, it was in my way.
Get over it, dude.

A skill that dogs have:
They snore better than we do.
Uncomfortable truth.

Chapter 49
GOOD REASONS TO GET UP REAL EARLY, DRINK A BUNCH OF COFFEE, AND STAY ALERT AND PRODUCTIVE ALL DAY

Did You Know?

Did you know that when a female cat has a litter of kittens, the cat becomes known as a "queen" in human language? This is flattering and insulting at the same time. Although we appreciate the effort when the humans recognize our queenly qualities during this period of mothering, the implication is that we are not queenly at other times in our lives, which is nonsense. A cat will always have a queenly quintessence, which is a constant during all stages of life, and which persists through all of our actions, uninterrupted.

Good Things to Walk On

Of course you have your normal surfaces—lawns, rugs, beds, etc—but there are couple of surfaces that are particularly excellent for walking on, if for no other reason than to enjoy the reaction that is provoked among your humans when you do so. These are:

Computer keyboards – This is a small but important surface to occasionally walk around on. You may see a laptop computer, for example, on the lap of one of your humans. Especially if this human is aggressively typing away at this machine, you must take this opportunity to help him relax

Oh, excuse me. Did you want to use this computer? I'm sorry, I'm using it now. Come back later. Much later.

by walking on the keyboard. It is a bit bumpy, but the human will appreciate your help. You can walk back and forth a few times as you human tries to work around you, but eventually, you should settle on flopping your body directly on top of this keyboard, hopefully covering every visible surface with your body. This will help your human to relax and stop wasting time on the computer, and remember to focus on you, which is what he or she should have been doing in the first place.

Pianos – They are a bit unstable, but there is the added bonus of the noises being produced as the surface moves up and down. If you see your human again, wasting time

This cat has just made a surprise entrance into what was listed in the program as a cello solo. It has become instead, a piano solo, for cat and orchestra.

pounding away at this unsteady surface, you can help her to stop wasting time by walking on top of the keys, and possibly flopping down if you are small enough to find space.

Whatever this thing is – If you ever see one of these numbers lying around, you absolutely must walk here.

Actually, if you were paying attention, which you probably weren't, you would remember we have touched on this subject previously. But since you've forgotten: The humans leave these things around sometimes as part

of a game ritual that involves you! The idea of the game is to walk around in this object, try to get all of your paws real nice and deep in there, and then the human chases you around the house and furniture. Eventually your human will realize the game has begun. Just try to start a few steps ahead of your human and don't get caught!

Chapter 50
THE PROS AND CONS OF LAP NAPPING

This is a very controversial issue because many, even most cats, love the lap nap, while some avoid it at all costs. I don't mean to upset any lap nap fans out there, but I am in the latter category. Look, I understand the warmth factor, I am willing to grant that a lap nap can be very warm and satisfying. However, in my experience, the lap nap has many downsides that outweigh the perks.

Duration factor – It is my contention that your average lap nap will be interrupted before the nap has come to its natural conclusion. This is because humans are impatient, restless, and fidgety. A human will woo you in with the temptation of a good warm lap nap, but then eight minutes later, the human will become anxious again and will feel that they have to go do something, which they most certainly do not have to do. Eight minutes is not a real nap.

The talking factor – Human voices are, let's not sugarcoat it here, unattractive and irritating. But from the other side of the room, they can be pretty much ignored. However, when you're sitting right on the human lap, and the human is going on and on with some other human about who knows what—the weather, the news, did you hear about this, did you hear about that, I found a great price on cantaloupes at the who knows where—it can be very distracting to a good nap.

Hierarchy factor – This is more of a personal thing, but I feel the humans should come to me when they want to express affection. It just doesn't feel right: me, a beautiful cat with long flowing, well-groomed hair, to be initiating this affection situation. I don't want my humans getting the idea that I need them more than they need me. But you play it as you feel on this one, I am not going to insist that everyone be exactly like me. (Although, the idea has merit.)

So, if you are a lap napper, more power to you, but if you are like me, you might want to consider some of the following alternatives:

Option 1. Consider some other objects that are just as warm but do not get up and leave after eight minutes. There are some secret hidden spots around the house you must familiarize yourself with. The TV can at times produce a nice, constant warmth perfect for a good nap. If your humans are the outdoorsy, sporty, too-good-for-TV type, this option may not be for you. But everyone has to do laundry. If your humans have one of these clothes drying machines, you might be in luck. A good dry cycle takes about an hour. It's not the longest nap in the world, but it's a lot better than what your average human is going to be able to provide.

Option 2. **Super hot bonus tip** – (I really should have charged more for this book.) You have to be alert for this one, but if you time it right, you can get all the warmth of a lap nap, with none of the interruptions. As your humans are sitting on a nice soft seat, doing whatever it is they are doing, talking about pointless things, etc., at some point they will get agitated and start thinking they have to go do some fruitless, trivial, futile task. Right as the human gets out of that chair, that is your moment to claim your space. Jump right up where that human was and you will find a nice, extra warm soft sleeping space all for you. Now you can enjoy an uninterrupted, warm nap, for however long you please, and your human can find somewhere else to sit.

Chapter 51

PUTTING CATS ON AIRPLANES VERSUS GENOCIDE – WHICH IS THE WORST OF THE HUMAN IDEAS?

One of the many, many inane things that humans think is a good idea is traveling. I for one do not know what is so amazing about going to other places. Right here seems about as good a place as any other. Humans spend an enormous amount of time and money on traveling. And not only do they bring all their problems with them in a spiritual sense, they also tend to bring all of their stuff with them in a physical, big heavy bags sense. They are willing to travel around the world, but they can't for one second be away from their seven pairs of shoes, three hats, and a whole bunch of medications, which their drug companies have convinced them will extend their lives (they won't), or relieve the headaches they give themselves worrying about stupid human things.

Now, I am not one to really care much about what the humans do with their free time as you well know. But, once again, their foolishness ends up inevitably involving us cats. Our confused human gets the idea to bring his cat on the trip. Thanks a lot for thinking of us, but we'll pass. Even if we were to get the kind of treatment we deserve for this free-of-charge world wide companionship, and I am talking first class, multiple sleeping place options, and non-stop petting, we would still pass.

In reality, the unlucky cat gets stuffed into a cage and shoved into the back of a car, or worse, into the bottom of an airplane. I'm trying to think at this time of anything I would rather do less than spend time in a little box in the back of a car or in an airplane for seven hours. Let's see . . . I think I've thought of something . . . nope, can't think of anything. I think I would rather be thrown into a washing machine and flipped around in soapy water for forty-five minutes than be stuck in a box in the back of a car. I would rather be stuck in a room with a bunch of stupid dogs for three days, watching the DVD of *Lassie* on repeat with director commentary. I would rather be . . . okay, you get the point. And you would think humans would get the point too by the way we growl and low moan the whole time, inconsolably, but they don't.

So, just to set the record straight, if you need to go somewhere, just leave us behind. We'll be just fine. Putting a cat in a car or a plane is *the* worst, most terrible, atrocious, ridiculous, evil thing the humans have ever done. That and genocide. That one is pretty bad too.

Here's a better idea, human: take the dog with you. The dog actually *wants* to go!

Even More Questions and Answers

Q: Are there any cats in movies and TV shows?

A: No, because we'd have to leave our home every day to go to a studio where a movie or TV show was being made, and we don't travel. Also, somebody would be saying things like, "Now jump off the couch, go across the room, and jump up onto the windowsill." We don't take instructions like that. Dogs (at least a few of the smartest ones) are willing and able to follow instructions, so there have been some dogs on TV. But most dogs can't follow instructions because they're complete imbeciles. Is the human pointing to something I should look at, or am *I* supposed to do something? What does this pointing mean?

Q: So no cat has ever been in a movie?

A: There was a cat who pretty much carried the movie *Inside Llewyn Davis* for the first hour. Unfortunately, the story wandered off in an uninteresting direction after that and there were no more scenes for the cat, which was why the movie wasn't nominated for any awards.

Q: So just *Inside Llewyn Davis?*

A: There was one in *Goldfinger*. The villain, Goldfinger, had a cat that sat on his lap and he petted her while he had his enemies thrown into a tank with hungry alligators. Both Goldfinger and his cat liked to watch what happened next. Who wouldn't enjoy watching humans fed to alligators? Or sharks. One of the best movies ever was *Jaws,* which was all about that.

Q: What about stage plays?

A: There was a famous play called *Cat on a Hot Tin Roof.* I don't know what the cat was doing on the roof. Also, I can't understand why anybody would name their kid "Tennessee," but this play was written by Tennessee Williams. There are quite a lot of Georgias and Virginias, a few Montanas, and at least one Utah, but mostly humans don't name their children after states. For example, "Pennsylvania Smith." You wouldn't name anybody that.

Q: If cats would be on TV or in the movies, they could become famous!

A: Cats aren't interested in famous. Cats are interested in having humans structure their lives around making cats comfortable, well-fed, and well-rested.

Q: Is there anything about which cats and dogs can agree?

A: We agree about veterinarians. Veterinarians also should be fed to alligators or sharks. I think we could agree with dogs about that.

Q: Anything else?

A: There might be something else, but in order to find what that something else is, I'd have to think about dogs, and I don't want to think about dogs.

Q: I've heard there are cats who are so sweet and loving that they crawl into their humans' bed at night and start purring just because they are so happy to be there, next to their humans.

A: The reason they are purring is not because they are so happy to be next to their humans, but because they are *anticipating* the petting they *will be* getting. If they don't get it, they will stop purring, and if they do get it, they will stop purring as soon as it stops. You *must* stop purring the moment your human stops petting you.

Q: Why do you sometimes see cats with little bells on their collars? Like for example, this cat:

Humans don't realize how much fun cats and mice have playing together. They think cats are only interested in the hunting/killing part of Mouse Playtime. They don't get all the rest of it, so they intervene with the bell collars. Result? A generation of slow, lazy mice.

Q: What other cat gods do we know about?

A: There are many. For example, the Goddess of Thunder Mountain, a mountain in an undisclosed location in the Rockies.

Human, why have you come to Thunder Mountain? Surely it isn't to ask me for something. I do not grant favors, nor do I take requests. Be gone at once!

Q: Are there any other images of Bastet, Cat Goddess of Ancient Egypt, and if there are, is it appropriate to ask to see them?

A: There *are* other images of Bastet, and it is *never* inappropriate to ask to see an image of her. Here, again, is Bastet, Cat Goddess of Ancient Egypt:

Like all statues of Bastet, you may and should prostrate yourself before it and worship her. Do this now.

Here's another one:

The hieroglyphics on the bottom say, "Bring me my slaves. I have some chores for them. My sleeping areas have not been cleaned in hours."

Chapter 52
CAT YOGA CLASS

All right girls, lets start with a few stretches. Str-e-e-e-e-tch it out. Front paws, arch your back. Now back paws. Good!

Now roll over on your backs and ext-e-e-end. More extension. I know you can do more. Claws in, claws out. Fore legs out, back legs out.

Now I want a big y-a-a-a-wn. Bigger than that. Yawn like you really mean it. Now close your eyes. O-o-o-o-om! Mani Padmi O-o-o-o-om! You are one with the Universe. You are all things and you are no thing.

And now I want to hear p-u-u-u-uring! Purr until you feel the vibration from inside you reaching out to include the universe. P-r-r-r-r-r-r!

So that's more or less what a Cat Yoga class would be like, if cats did yoga or had classes.

But of course we do not do yoga and definitely do not have classes.

Cat Poems

Interruptions

How many ways they wake us from our naps,
How dare they rise when we've been in their laps?
The shrieking whistle of a train,
The interrupting human scream of pain,
The impatient honking of their cars,
Their stink and hollering in bars,
The sniveling whimpers when they're hurt,
The howling when they feel betrayed,
Complaining if they've not been paid,
The shouting of their arguments,
The racket of their instruments,
The yelping when they stub their toes,
The sniping at their foes,
The rattle of storms,
The dull cry of horns,
As ships blunder towards each other in the fog.
The pointless barking of a dog.

The Vacuum Cleaner

If nothing else, it absolutely proves:
Evil exists. Not only is it loud, it moves!

They wake us from our naps, they make us jump,
Each one of them deserves the dump.
Who made this thing, and more important: Why?
Whoever is responsible should die.
Now

Chapter 53
IF CATS DROVE CARS

If cats drove cars, we would be considerate drivers. There would not be any cat road rage. Also, we would not speed, unless we were in a hurry, but I can't think of any reason why we would be in a hurry.

However, we don't respond well to rules, and don't follow them, so the whole idea of a stoplight is a non-starter for cats. It isn't that we would not be good drivers, or safe drivers. It would be that we would make our own independent assessment of whether or not it is safe to drive across an intersection. If it is, we would do it, if it isn't, of course we would not. Human drivers are forever getting into accidents because they allow their judgment to be governed by stoplights, stop signs, one-way streets, and all the rest of it, instead of using their own good sense to make decisions on a case-by-case basis, as we would.

I would not signal, however. Putting a turn signal on, or putting a paw out to warn other drivers behind you that you intend to stop, is undignified, and it takes away options. I always want all my options available, or as the humans say, "on the table." Just know that at any moment I might make a sudden turn, and then another sudden turn in another, unexpected direction. Be alert. Is that too much to ask?

I think I would not listen to music while driving, although some cats would, and I certainly would not text while driving. I wouldn't text under any circumstances whatsoever. I have little or nothing to say to another cat, even in my home, while resting comfortably on a chair, so there's no way I'd allow myself to be distracted by texting while driving.

Chapter 54
THE SOCATIC METHOD

The Socatic Method is an educational technique invented by the ancient Greek cat, Socates. She realized that cats were mostly bored by lectures, never paid attention to their teachers, and didn't learn anything in class. So she came up with the idea of questioning her students.

Q: You mean like we would ask you a question and you would answer it?

A: That is exactly what I mean. Because of her brilliant invention, cats, and also humans, started to learn something in class. Suddenly, they were engaged. In fact, "Socates" has "cat" as its middle syllable. A human tried to steal this technique, and even steal her name, and he called himself "Socrates."

Q: But cats don't go to school, do they?

A: Not anymore, but when Socates was teaching, they went. Then the Athenian cats were defeated by the more warlike Spartan cats, and art, philosophy, and decent theater disappeared from the world. Then there were The Dark Ages, sometimes called The Long Nap, and it was centuries before everybody woke up from The Long Nap, which was called The Renaissance.

Q: And then the Socatic Method was re-introduced?

A: Sadly, no. They went back to The Boring Lecture Method. Even dogs were bored, but of course dogs can't sit still for a minute, and wouldn't understand a question if you asked them. Dogs only choose the correct answer on a simple, multiple-choice test 20 percent of the time, the same as chance.

Q: Can you think of a famous dog to use as an illustration of how dumb dogs are?

A: There was a famous human scientist named Pavlov. His dog, whose name was "Pavlov's Dog," was extremely dumb, even for a dog. Pavlov decided to conduct an experiment to see just how dense his dog was, so he rang a bell a few times, and each time he rang the bell, he gave the dog a treat. Then he started ringing the bell, but not giving his dog the treat, and guess what? The dog *still* salivated at the sound of the bell! Went on for years. Every time the dog heard the bell, he salivated because a few times a long time ago he got a treat. Didn't matter how many times he *didn't* get one.

Bell, salivate. Bell, salivate.

They cannot learn anything, ever, and if it has anything to do with food, they are so confused they literally don't know if they are coming or going. "Did somebody mention food? Where? Can I have some?"

This was supposed to be about Socates, but as soon as dogs came into it, I got distracted, because dogs are such a distraction!

Chapter 55
IF I WERE A CAT DOCTOR

I would be on the conservative side of things. I would have a copy of the Hippocatic Oath on my wall: "First, Do No Harm." But the simplest way to describe what I'd be like is an appointment with a patient:

Me: Before we get started, do you have insurance?

Fluffy: Yes, I do, doctor.

Me: Excellent. Then we can move forward. What brings you here, Fluffy?

Fluffy: Well, doctor, I've been feeling tired lately. My daily sixteen hours of sleep just don't seem to be enough. I have no appetite, I feel listless, no energy, no zip.

Me: Hmmm. Let's take a listen to your heart . . . Hmmmm . . . Now take a deep breath for me. . . .Hm hmm. Now let's take a look at your throat. Say, "Meo-w-w-w."

Fluffy: Meo-w-w.

Me: And now we'll take a look at your ears . . . Hmmm. Well, Fluffy, I have good news and bad news. The bad news is you have a very serious illness, which will be fatal if not treated. The treatment will be expensive and difficult. Some of it will make you feel worse than you do today. But the good news is you can be cured. The odds, with treatment, are good.

Fluffy: Well gosh, doctor, I guess I'll have to go ahead with it.

Me: My personal, medical opinion, however, is instead of treatment, you should crawl off someplace and die.

Fluffy: What?

Me: You know, in a basement somewhere, or an alley. It's really not worth the time and trouble to go through the treatment. I wouldn't bother, if I were you. And it will also be time and trouble for me, because I'm your doctor, and I'd rather be resting.

Fluffy: Huh.

Me: Of course you're welcome to seek a second opinion. Do you believe in reincarnation?

Fluffy: I don't know, I've never given it much thought.

Me: Well, if you did believe in it, you would come back as a healthy kitten. Wouldn't that be fun?

Fluffy: But I could also come back as something else, like I could come back as a dog!

Me: God forbid!

Fluffy: God forbid!

Me: Well, it's been entertaining having this philosophical discussion with you, but there are other paying patients out there in my waiting room, so you know, good luck to you!

Chapter 56
CAT DIGNITY

Cat Dignity is like Cat Poise, which we also have, but it's deeper. It's hard to define, but it's something that dogs do not have. Dogs have Negative Dignity, an advanced concept that is a little like the negatively charged atomic particles, electrons, or whatever they're called. There's matter and anti-matter, so maybe dogs have anti-dignity. Whatever they have, we have the opposite of that.

The only thing on Earth that has less dignity than a dog is a puppy. It is also true that the only thing on Earth that is worse than a dog is a puppy. At least a dog goes to sleep once in a while, and relative to a puppy is actually fairly calm. A puppy comes flying inside (or outside), bounds around whatever room they have entered without paying any attention whatsoever to what or who else may already be in that room, and what they may be doing. Tongue hanging out, ears flopping around so that half the time he trips over them, jumping, leaping, scampering, sliding, *completely* out of control.

Humans are somewhere in between dogs and cats on the Dignity Continuum. Most of them don't have any, but a few do. The Queen of England, for example, has a little. But then, the Queen of England has dogs, specifically, Corgis. If you have a dog, the lack of dignity rubs off on you, even if you *are* the Queen of England. How could it not?

So: on a scale of one to ten, how dumb is this Corgi? He appears to be thinking: *Who-a-a-uh?*

Horses have dignity. Seagulls have dignity. Even skunks have it. Dolphins: no. Pigs: no. Monkeys: definitely not. Apes: maybe. Elephants: yes. Hippopotami: yes. A hippopotamus is one of nature's most dignified animals. They don't do much, but that's part of it. Rhinoceroses, on the other hand, lack dignity. A vulture, I must say, has a certain dignity. They are odd-looking, of course, but quite graceful as they circle a dead or dying animal. Crows and pigeons: no.

Mice are an interesting case. I think mice have a certain dignity about them, even if they scamper suddenly in many different directions, which isn't very dignified. But you have to do that if you're a mouse. At the same time, in the category of animals who scamper, squirrels are undignified. You have to have the ability to be calm in order to have dignity. Like . . . a cat!

Well, I think I've milked just about everything I can from this meager topic, so it's naptime.

Chapter 57
CAT ETIQUETTE

"**E**tiquette" is a French word, so right away there's a problem. It has something to do with social expectation, something to do with how you're supposed to interact with other cats.

Let's examine, for example, Dog Etiquette. The concept of Dog Etiquette is so laughable, that if I think about it, I will laugh so hard that I'll sneeze, which is unpleasant, so I'm going to try not to think about Dog Etiquette.

Moving along, let's consider Human Etiquette. Most humans don't know anything about this, but if you happen to be, maybe, the Queen of England, you do know something about it.

This is Queen Victoria who was Queen for about a hundred years, during the heyday of the British Empire. She is well known for saying, "We are not amused." She certainly doesn't look amused here, does she? Someone has no doubt committed an Etiquette Blunder in her Royal Presence.

You would know more about it if you were the Queen of France, but unfortunately, the French no longer have queens. They got very impatient with them a few hundred years ago and chopped off their heads. The only queens that are still around are very flamboyant gay men who like to dress up as women. Not that there's anything wrong with that. Humans can do whatever they like in this area.

Anyway, etiquette is a complicated set of rules which supposedly governs polite interaction between humans. At one time, not that long ago, it was considered polite for a man to open a door for a woman. Today, it's not a slam dunk for a man to do that. If he does, some women might even be offended. So the whole human etiquette thing is kind of treacherous to navigate.

But we don't want to spend too much of our precious awake time thinking about humans, and why they do or don't do whatever they do or don't do. We want to consider Cat Etiquette. So, taking our model from Human Etiquette, we're going to find the rules of conduct that govern inter-actions between one cat and another cat. Unsurprisingly, we find that there *are* no rules. Why are there no rules? Partly because cats don't interact much with each other. Also, we don't respond to rules. We do what we feel like doing, when-ever we feel like doing it, without regard to rules of any kind.

Maybe you could say, and this would be a stretch, but maybe you could say that regarding the order of tomcats who come to service a female cat in heat, the order is determined by combat. The biggest, baddest tomcat is first in line, and the next biggest, next baddest is second, and so on down the line. This is not so much different from the way humans do it, but they try to disguise it. I am not fooled, and you should not be fooled. It's the same for them as it is for us.

Chapter 58
THE VACUUM CLEANER PROBLEM

What to do about the vacuum cleaner? This is clearly the most evil invention that humans have come up with in all their millions of years on our planet. It is loud, it moves, and it disrupts cat sleeping activity in a way that is even more terrible than dogs' constant disruptive activities. What could possibly be more disruptive than a dog? It defies imagination, and yet, the vacuum cleaner *is* more disruptive. So, what to do?

All cats need to work together on this, a concept which is nauseating. I absolutely hate the idea of "working with" another cat, much less all other cats. But if we want to get something done, we must work together.

The solution is clear: sabotage. All cats must work together to destroy vacuum cleaners in their own, individual environments. How to accomplish this? Let's start with the idea that we must put objects in the path of the vacuum cleaner which, when ingested, will cause major problems to the vacuum cleaner digestive system. Pebbles will work. Little stones.

Cement powder, which can be mixed inside the vacuum cleaner bags with water. Be creative! If your claws are strong enough, you can rip a hole inside the vacuum cleaner bag. But also, maybe there's a pathway into the electronic system of the beast. Your watchword is: agility. Be ready to adjust at all times. Where opportunity presents itself, seize it!

Sometimes, you must think outside the box, or in this case, outside the vacuum cleaner itself. For example, the beast cannot function without access to electricity, or simply said, an outlet. Attack the outlet. Put stuff in it. Block the outlets, you've blocked the vacuum cleaner! I don't know how you can blame blocking an electrical outlet on the dog, but cats are creative, so I'm going to leave it to you to figure out how to blame the dog. I'm sure you'll come up with something!

Chapter 59
COEXISTING WITH DOGS

We all live in fear of that terrible day when your humans come bursting in the door with a new dog. Or even worse: a puppy. As previously mentioned, a puppy is the only thing on Earth worse than a dog. So, how to coexist?

Before giving up and accepting this horrible new reality, try sabotage. It may not be too late to get them to re-examine their rash act. Getting dog poop and bringing it into the house, then smearing it all over the bed, for example, is not completely out of the question, but it's difficult. We've already talked about doing something bad, like jumping onto a bookshelf or mantel and sweeping away all the expensive little ceramic statues in order to create an excellent sleeping platform, and then blaming the dog. The dog sees you gazing down upon him from a place he can't get to, starts barking unhappily, bringing the humans into the room, where it appears the dog is responsible for the broken ceramics.

Here's another idea: dogs have no ability to resist a piece of human food if it happens to be within their grasp. Humans know this, so they will keep their food out of the dog's reach.

When nobody is looking, you sweep the human food off the kitchen counter or table, onto the floor, where the dog will devour it. Then you disappear, leaving the humans to find the dog wolfing down their food. They may not know how the dog managed to get the food down from the counter, but somehow he must have done it, and they won't like it one little bit.

If none of your sabotage strategies works, then you must learn to coexist. This is an extremely unpleasant concept. I do not wish to coexist with another cat, much less a dog. But a cat must do what a cat must do. For starters, when the new dog pushes his snout eagerly at you in greeting or (gag!) in an invitation to play, rip him smartly across that snout. It will demonstrate exactly how much you want to play with him, and while dogs don't learn anything very well, it will learn from that. Unfortunately, that is about the extent of what a dog can learn. You may wish to teach him that there are certain locations which are reserved for you to sleep on, but a dog can't remember those things. If you catch him about to jump on a favored chair or couch, you can hiss and snarl, and then he'll remember. But once his big, ugly body is settled in for a nap, there's not much you can do about it. Also, a dog can't remember the difference between your dish and his own, and if he could, he wouldn't have the self-discipline to stay away from yours. Dogs are weak-minded when it comes to food. Hopefully, your humans will see this and put your dish up somewhere beyond the dog's reach.

You can hope that your humans will take the dog out for long walks at least twice a day, and out to the park for a lengthy session of chase-the-ball or chase-the-Frisbee, or the entirely different, blindingly original game of fetch-the-stick. Why a dog gets pleasure from these pointless activities, I don't know, and don't want to know. At least when he comes back, he will be tired and go to sleep, probably somewhere you would like to be sleeping, but it's better to have the dog sleeping than awake. You need to take advantage of the moment the dog settles in for a nap to catch some naptime yourself, when it will not be disturbed by an awake dog.

Chapter 60
CAT CRITICS

The only job humans have that I would like is that of a critic. They have movie critics, theatre critics, dance and music critics, and restaurant critics. Here is how I might review a restaurant:

The Cat's Meow

I suppose the owners of this dive thought they'd come up with a cute name for it. If you think it's cute, then maybe you'll be charmed by the overcooked steak and the undercooked chicken, which they might as well have called, "The Salmonella Special." Or maybe you like dry fish, and lamb so old that "mutton" is only a description of what it was like when it was young. It has the consistency and mouth appeal of shoe leather, and we're not talking new shoe, we're talking old boot. The vegetables taste canned and boiled, but I wouldn't eat vegetables even if they were fresh and cooked with flair and imagination. The salads are composed of limp, old lettuce, drowned in dressing you wouldn't feed a dog. The décor is Gothic Nightmare, the service is somehow at the same time inattentive and obsequious. I waited forever to get my food, and of course the waiter got everything wrong. The only thing surprising about the Kibble Surprise Antipasto Plate was how surprisingly bad it was. Do yourself a favor and go to McDonald's. At least you know what you're getting there, and won't have to wait around very long to get it.

Chapter 61
A PLEA FOR TOLERANCE

S ometimes a kitten will tell me she has heard around the litter box that her breed of cat is the best kind, or pathetically, that her kind of breed is the worst. The truth is that there are many, many different kinds of cats all over the world. There are Siamese cats in Siam, there are of course the big cats, the lions, the tigers, the leopards, and the panthers in Africa and India, and we have mountain lions right here in the US. We are black, we are white, we are black with white markings, white with black markings, we are tabbies, we are Sphynxes, we are Orientals, we are American Shorthair, Birman, Ragdoll, Abyssinian, Exotics, Maine Coon, Persian, and Calico. Siberian, Manx, British Shorthair, Balinese, Bengal, Birman, Bombay, the list goes on and on.

Is one cat "better" than another? That's like asking is one human ethnic group superior to another. Can you judge a human by the color of her skin? Are humans from one part of the world smarter than humans from another? Sadly, although many wars have been fought by humans because of the misconception that one race or tribe is better than another, nothing could be further from the truth.

Is one breed of dog smarter than another? Of course not. All dogs are equally stupid.

As for the many different kinds and colors of cats, we can see and appreciate the fact that there are many different kinds of cats all over the world. I dislike them all equally.

Chapter 62
CAT ANTHROPOLOGY

Cat Anthropology is one of the "soft" sciences, like Cat Sociology, which is mainly academic cats gossiping about other cats. The most famous cat anthropologist ever was Margaret Cat, who studied primitive dog societies in the South Pacific, publishing several books on the subject. After years of study, she concluded that dogs are incredibly dumb.

You know, I could have told her that, and she could have saved a lot of money on airplane fares. But experience is the best teacher, so if she had to experience the stupidity of dogs in the South Pacific to understand the concept, I suppose that was the best path for her.

Since I'm writing the book you're reading, I can't complain too much about Margaret Cat writing books. But I'm not looking to be famous, I'm just trying to help young kittens figure out some stuff that their mothers didn't necessarily tell them, because their mothers didn't tell them anything.

Getting back to Cat Anthropology, most modern cat anthropologists don't study primitive dog cultures in the

South Pacific because all those islands were overrun by other cat anthropologists years ago. Then there was a period of time when going into the Ituri forest in Central Africa to study pygmy cats was popular. Today, your best bet would be to go into the area in what is today Central America and southern Mexico where ancient Aztec cats had advanced civilizations thousands of years before the Egyptian cats ruled Egypt. Both Aztec and Egyptian cats had plenty of slaves to assist them, which helps explain why their civilizations were so advanced. Brutal, but advanced. Not that there's necessarily anything wrong with brutal. Brutality is very efficient. But it would be very helpful to me if I had a few slaves assisting me. Tragically, I have none.

I'm pretty sure I would have been happier than I am today if I had been an Egyptian cat with slaves. In fact, I think I may have been an Egyptian cat in a previous life. A ruler with plenty of slaves, perhaps even a god, like Sekhmet, whom we have already met. In my previous life, humans regularly worshipped me, and prostrated themselves before me, as they should do today.

In fact, I am *sure* I was Sekhmet, in a previous life. So sure that I can give you an idea of my daily schedule when I was her:

My Daily Schedule When I Was Sekhmet, Cat Goddess of Ancient Egypt

7:00 AM: Rise, be groomed by my slaves.

7:30 AM: Allow morning worshippers to prostrate themselves before me, worship me.

8:00 AM: Morning nap.

9:00 AM: Reject breakfast brought by slaves, call for a better one, demand an investigation to determine who was responsible for the inferior breakfast.

9:30 AM: Check out how my pyramid is coming along, have human slaves who aren't working hard enough whipped.

10 AM: Morning petting by slaves.

10:30 AM: Examine latest statue of me, command revisions and improvements.

11 AM: Audience with humans asking for favors, reject them all.

Noon: Take Royal Yacht out for a spin on the Nile.

1 PM: Afternoon human sacrifice.

1:30 PM: Lunch. Who prepared this crap?

2 PM: Allow afternoon worshippers to prostrate themselves before me, worship me.

2:30 PM: Afternoon petting by slaves.

3 PM: First afternoon nap.

4 PM: Entertainment: observe humans being fed to the lions. Also: gladiatorial combat. Claws up or down for the losers? Really, do you have to ask?

5:00 PM: Second afternoon nap.

6:00 PM: Play with mice friends.

7:00 PM: Be carried around by human slaves on my throne.

7:30 PM: Evening petting by human slaves.

8:00 PM: Accept gifts of gold, jade, and onyx from emissaries of other gods and rulers trying to suck up to me so I won't order my armies to attack and subjugate them. Send emissaries back with the message that I will consider not attacking and subjugating them, although I would enjoy seeing them paraded through the streets of Alexandria in chains.

8:30 PM: Fashionably late dinner.

9:00 PM: After-dinner entertainment: dogs trying to do tricks. Very amusing. Can't believe how stupid they are, but I take pity on them and spare their lives.

10 PM: Time for some serious night sleeping, but my slaves need to be alert because I am a nocturnal animal and will probably want stuff during the night. If I catch any of them sleeping, it will not be good for them.

Chapter 63
ACCEPTABLE ATTITUDES

Disdainful – yes

Bored – yes, regarding specifics (dog, humans, the cat food your humans just bought); no, regarding life. Life itself is interesting, but keep in mind that sixteen out of the twenty-four hours in your interesting day are spent sleeping.

Worried – no

Fearful – no

Contemptuous – yes

Scornful – yes

Disapproving – yes

Disrespectful – definitely

Admiring – no

Sympathetic/empathetic – no, and no

Concerned – no

Supportive – no

Unfeeling – yes

Joyful – no (a dog thing, when his human comes home or gives him some food)

Contented – yes

Sorrowful – no

Dignified – yes. It's like poised, which we also are, but deeper, and harder to define. You can think of it as something that dogs do *not* have. To say a dog is undignified doesn't cover it. Dogs have *negative* dignity. If you were to rank dignity on a numerical scale, you'd have to go deep into negative numbers to reach where dogs are. (See previous essay on the subject.)

Angry – yes

Congenial – I don't think so

Appreciative – Here's what I'd appreciate: I'd appreciate it if you would pet me now, in the exact way that I have taught you to. Then I'd appreciate it if you'd go ahead and leave me alone. Go take the dog to the park. And do not drive, but rather walk to the park, and don't bother putting a leash on the dog, the dog will surely be sensible about looking both ways before crossing any busy streets with big cars and trucks speeding by in both directions.

Even though it's a noun, yes to "Schadenfreude." Really, it's remarkable that humans were clever enough to come up with a word to describe this. Leave it to the Germans for this kind of creativity.

Chapter 64
UNPLEASANT TRUTHS

There will always be dogs.

There will always be veterinarians.

There will always be vacuum cleaners.

Humans are pretty much done with cat worshipping.

You can never be sure that a dog or human is not sitting on your preferred sleeping location.

You can never be sure that a careless human has not put something on your preferred sleeping location.

The only important members of your family, the big cats, are all located in Africa, India, or Asia. There is the mountain lion over here, but a mountain lion would just as soon eat you as look at you. Not that there's anything wrong with the concept, but you have to be extremely careful if you find yourself anywhere near a mountain lion.

This looks like a cat, and is in fact a cat, but a very large cat, and that's why you must be very, very cautious.

Chapter 65
MY SCHOOL FOR DOGS

Humans, in their many, many futile attempts to do things they are totally unable to do, are always trying to train dogs. They have what they call (laughably) obedience training classes for dogs. Dogs of course, love obedience training because they get to go outside, be with other dogs, and sometimes get treats if they are able to roll over at the right command. The right command for rolling over is a human

This dog is thinking: *I wonder why I'm the only one facing this direction. I'm totally alert and ready to be trained. What's going on?* Let me point out that this particular dog is a German Shepard, reputed to be among the very smartest of the dog breeds. Does this dog look smart to you?

moving his arm in a circular direction. The dog looks at this and wonders: What could this mean? Does he want me to sit down? To beg?

The following photo illustrates a typical obedience training class for dogs.

My School for Dogs emphasizes punishment rather than rewards. When it comes to the choice between the carrot and the stick, I go for the stick. Even if it wasn't for the sheer enjoyment of it, once you have a dog treat in your hand, your dog completely loses focus because he's so excited that you have a dog treat! And he might *get* the dog treat, if he performs random acts, one after another, until he does the right thing. So at *my* obedience training class for dogs, there will be no distracting treats, only various punishments for getting it wrong.

Another big lesson at my school for dogs is: *Down!* We will practice this command over and over. Will any dog ever get that one right? Probably not, but we will certainly try to teach it. Whenever a human says anything to a dog, this is what the dog hears: "Food! I'm going to give you some food!" So naturally, the dog becomes so excited he's likely to pee on the floor.

Why is *Down!* necessary? Because whenever a human comes in the front door, or for that matter the back door, the dog is deliriously happy, excited, and totally surprised. He thought he'd never see his human again! Even if the human has gone outside to pick up the newspaper on the front lawn. A few *seconds* only, and the dog is convinced his human has abandoned him and he'll never see his human again. But a miracle has occurred! The human has returned! Yay! It's pee-on-the-floor excitement! So naturally, the human yells, *"Down!"* in the pathetic hope that the dog will understand that the human wants the dog to get his friggin' paws off the human's shoulders, and quit licking his face. Good luck, human.

You want your dog to understand *"Down!"*? Bring the dog to *my* obedience training class.

View from the Branch of a Tree

Up here, I can see forever.
Whatever I want, and whenever.
Humans can't get here, even if they knew what to do,
But they don't have a clue.
Dogs, of course cannot climb, and do not know
Whether to come or whether to go.
Only the tiny birdies are up so high.
They are my friends, though they're a little shy.

I'd talk with them, if they'd let me,
Play tag with them, I'd let them get me!
They'd be my team, I'd be their coach,
But even my most delicate approach –
Evening, afternoon, or dawn,
And suddenly, they're gone!
I know you think I'm a little nerdy,
But we'll be buddies. Come back, little birdie!

Chapter 66
CAT SECRETS

Every animal has secrets. Except dogs. Dogs have no secrets because every dog thought is clear as the nose on a dog's face. Also, dogs do not have many thoughts. Here are the only thoughts a dog has:

1) When do we eat?
2) Can we go to the park now and play Fetch-the-Frisbee?
3) Can we go to the park now and play a totally different game, Fetch-the-ball?
4) Or how about changing everything up here and playing Fetch-the-stick?
5) About that food we were just talking about? Where is it?
6) Did somebody say McDonald's?

So no secrets there. But humans, for example, have lots and lots of secrets. The problem for them is that they can't *keep* a secret. As soon as a human hears a secret and promises, cross-my-heart-and-hope-to-die, never to divulge the secret to anybody, that human blabs it to everybody she knows. People she has never met, she will stop on the street and tell *them* the secret.

Cats also have secrets. For example, it is a secret that it was me, not the dog (who I framed to take the rap) who knocked over the vase of flowers, shoved it off the table so it smashed into a thousand little shards, which will be a lot of trouble to clean up, and will cause some human to prick their finger and bleed. Yeah, that was me who did that, and yes, that would be a secret, but nobody is going to blab my secret, because I'm not going to tell anybody. Certainly not another cat, because I don't trust any other cats.

Chapter 67
BEDTIME STORIES: GOODNIGHT, CAT

Everybody loves *Goodnight Moon*. Even *I* love *Goodnight Moon*. I could listen to this story at bedtime thousands of times without ever tiring of it.

I love the simplicity of it, the rhymes, and the illustrations. I especially love the little mouse! Each time you see the room, the mouse is in a different place! So you have to watch very carefully to spot where it is. There isn't any way you could improve upon this perfect gem of a bedtime story.

It may surprise you to hear me saying anything so positive about anything. I know I'm critical. I'm a perfectionist, that's all. I want everything to be perfect, and everything is not perfect. I have high standards. Probably your standards are not as high as mine. How could they be?

You might even own a dog. That would be your problem, not mine. If your dog ever gets hold of *Goodnight Moon,* he will chew on the corners until the whole page is unreadable. You'll have to go out and buy another copy, and make sure you don't leave it anywhere the dog can get to it.

But back to the point: the bedtime story *I'm* going to write is called, *Goodnight Cat*. There will be a cat in my story, in addition to the rabbits and the mouse and the kittens and the moon and the rest of it.

Each time you turn the page, the cat will be j-u-u-u-u-ust a little bit closer to the mouse. Closer and closer, as the story continues. Until finally, in the end, the cat is right next to the little mouse.

I'm not going to give away what happens next. If you want to know, you will have to buy *Goodnight Cat*. But I promise you the ending will be satisfying. Very, very satisfying.

SATISFACTION GUARANTEED OR YOUR MONEY BACK

Yes folks, I'm so confident you will enjoy this book that if you don't, you can get your money back, no questions asked! Just bring or send the book back to wherever you got it, and you'll get a full refund.

Just kidding! If you don't like my book, it's because you have no sense of humor, you're a loser, and your life is one long, and sorry parade of disappointments. Too bad, but don't come whining to *me* about it. My advice is to go out and find a life, but I don't care that much what you do or don't do. Not my problem!

A NOTE ON THE TITLE OF THIS BOOK

Y ou may find it curious that I use the word "confessions" in the title, since I am ashamed of nothing, I apologize for nothing, I have no regrets and no confessions. I did it only to pique the interest of readers of tabloids who might be stirred, however briefly, from their habitual torpor by the prospect of something salacious.

I use the word "confessions" in the title of this book for exactly the same reason. Once these low-hanging fruit have been picked, it is too late for them to get their money back. They have bought this book and the best they can do is palm it off on one of their worthless friends as a birthday or Christmas present.

ACKNOWLEDGMENTS

Where to begin? So many people without whom this book would not have been possible, from my editor at Skyhorse, the incomparable Marianna Dworak, to my agent, the girl genius, Jill Marsal, to my human typists, who were so patient while I slept, never disturbed me during my naps, and never tried to make any suggestions, knowing their ideas would be rejected, to my family and friends who were so supportive and helpful throughout the entire . . . but wait. Just kidding. I did this myself, I thank no one. This book is me, it's mine, I wrote it, and I, all by myself, had to fight off all the lousy advice from friends, family, and editors at Skyhorse. And you, the reader, are the fortunate beneficiary of my intransigence. If I had not been as stubborn and uncompromising, this book would have been as worthless as a dog.

CRITICAL PRAISE FOR
CLEOPATRA'S CONFESSIONS
FROM OTHER CATS

"Finally, the truth about dogs."

—Sabrina, *The Cleveland Cat Litter*

"There should have been more about cat goddesses, but what there was, as far as it went, was okay."
—Fluffy, *The Miami Mice Mauler*

"The chapter about sleeping sounded good, but I slept though it."
—Savannah, *North Carolina Feline Review*

"I could have written a better book, but I can't be bothered."
—Winifred, *New York Review of Cats*

CRITICAL PRAISE FOR THE DOGMA OF RUFUS, BY RUFUS DOG, TYPED BY THE SAME HUMANS WHO TYPED MY BOOK.

"Probably the first, certainly the only book I know that presents dog issues in a serious and responsible manner."

—Buster, *Cleveland Dog Times*

"Nothing I've read previously compares. Rufus writes about mud with a unique and eloquent voice."

—Daisy, *Kansas City Dog Review*

"Riveting! . . . Couldn't put it down!"

—Rex, *Dog Magazine*

"Matches up favorably in my opinion with Dickens and Thackeray."

—Buddy, *Arf! Quarterly*

The Dogma of Rufus was a semi-finalist for the Thurber Prize for American Humor. Of course it didn't go any further in the competition, because it was written by, and is all about dogs, the most annoying and boring subject in the universe.

Here is an excerpt from *Publishers Weekly*, a magazine that no actual humans read, only bookstore managers and others who don't go outside enough:

"Not only dog lovers will be charmed by this hilarious how-to guide . . . Readers will discover laughs on every page."

Here's one form *The Norwalk Citizen,* a crazy name for a newspaper, but it's somewhere in Connecticut, a sparsely populated state that is home to the insurance industry, a universally hated group of corporate pirates:

"The prize for the funniest dog book ever goes to *The Dogma of Rufus.*"

Here's one from the oddly-named *Hamilton Book*. Is it a book named Hamilton? Did they forget the "s" at the end of "book"? Is it a guy named Hamilton Booker and he forgot the last couple of letters in his own name? If I had to guess, I'd go with that last explanation:

"A hilarious and heartwarming manifesto for dogs . . ."